Champions
in
the
Wilderness

Champions in the Wilderness

FIFTY-TWO DEVOTIONS TO GUIDE AND STRENGTHEN EMERGING OVERCOMERS

Bob Santos

SEARCH FOR ME MINISTRIES, INC.
INDIANA, PA

Champions in the Wilderness
Fifty-Two Devotions to Guide and Strengthen Emerging Overcomers
By Bob Santos

Cover Design: Nathan Miller
Interior Design: Sean McGaughran

Published by SfMe Media
A Division of Search for Me Ministries, Inc.
865 School Street
Indiana, PA 15701-2911
www.sfme.org

Printed in the United States of America

Library of Congress Control Number: 2013908128

ISBN: 978-1-937956-01-1

To the faithful individuals who have stood with us through prayer and financial partnership as we have navigated our own wilderness journey in getting Search for Me Ministries established.

CONTENTS

Stage Three - Finding Rest, Purpose, and Security in Desolate Places

Stage Four - Journeying with a Purpose

INTRODUCTION

Imagine you have the opportunity to attend the diving competition at the Summer Olympics. The crowd buzzes with excitement as the world's elite divers bounce gracefully from the platform with hardly a splash in the water below. Suddenly, the audience gasps as one particular diver walks to the platform. There appears a young man dressed in full gear for a downhill skiing outing! *Click, clack, click, clack,* you hear as his long skis bang against the diving platform with each fateful step. Apart from the ill-prepared diver, everyone present quickly recognizes that the scenario will not end well.

What does such an absurd illustration have to do with a devotional titled, *Champions in the Wilderness*? More than we may realize. Many of us in the Western church have developed the erroneous mentality that fruitful service to God is limited to only a few elite individuals. The rest are spectators who, from a safe distance, applaud—or criticize—the superstars. Yet, we are not merely onlookers in the arena of life—we are the participants! And our God is the all-wise coach whose goal is always to groom spiritual champions for heaven's glory.

Throughout the Bible, we find stories of men and women who, for one reason or another, found themselves in the midst of a wilderness experience. Whether or not the desolate territory they traversed was a literal wasteland is immaterial; each set of circumstances pointed toward a greater spiritual reality. More often than not, their response to lonely and adverse situations became the factor that determined who emerged as a champion and who sank miserably into defeat.

BIBLICAL TYPOLOGY

It is here that understanding the difference between the Old Testament and the New Testament becomes invaluable. The Old (Testament) is full of biblical *types*—physical examples used to illustrate spiritual truths later to be presented in the New. A sacrificial lamb from the book of Leviticus, for example, was a type of the New Covenant sacrifice of Christ's death on the cross. The illustration from the Old gives us a better grasp of the New.

Under the Old Covenant, men like Joshua and David reigned over *physical* enemies. They went to war, sometimes against giants, and always emerged overwhelming victors highly favored by God. Under the New Covenant, our foes are *spiritual* in nature. We are now called to reign over spiritual darkness, including the darkness of sin. A New Covenant champion rules over pride, despair, bitterness, and a host of other spiritual enemies that try to destroy us from the inside out.

SCRIPTURAL EXAMPLES

As any Christian would expect, Jesus Christ shines as our example of the greatest champion of the faith to ever walk this earth. Right after being water baptized, Jesus received a powerful affirmation from His heavenly Father (see Matthew 3-4). Strangely, rather than immediately beginning His ministry, Jesus then was led by the Holy Spirit into a barren wilderness. Victorious over temptation and fleshly desires, Jesus emerged forty days later and launched the most powerful ministry this world has ever seen.

In contrast to Christ's stellar example, we read in the first books of the Bible about a generation of Israelites whom God delivered from cruel bondage in Egypt, but who perished in the wilderness. Clueless to the fact that they were the participants in the arena of life, they responded with complaining and unbelief. Mired in confusion, they turned back to the idols of Egypt; the result of which was harsh judgment in multiple forms. Their God was by no means pleased with their unbelief. Only two men, Joshua and Caleb, emerged as champions from that particular wilderness experience.

Jesus Christ, the Son of Man, stood tall after being tested and proven in the wilderness, while the exodus generation of Israelites wallowed in self-pity and unbelief. Between the extreme examples of Jesus and those who came out of Egypt, we read of no small number of men and women who, by no choice of their own, were compelled to navigate adverse circumstances through desolate spiritual territory. Many—but not all—rose to the challenge.

Abraham wandered through the wilderness, waiting twenty-five years for his promised son to be born. Joseph was rejected and sold into slavery by his family. Moses spent forty years as a shepherd in a barren land because of his own failure. David found himself driven into isolation by King Saul. Daniel spent all of his adult life serving idolatrous kings in a foreign land. Jonah ran from God. The Apostle Paul lived for fourteen years faithfully serving God in obscurity before effectively beginning his ministry.

THE VALUE OF A SPIRITUAL WILDERNESS

Personally, I have spent much more time in spiritual wilderness territory than I would ever have imagined, but in spite of the often unpleasant nature of the wilderness, God has used those times to help form me into the image of Christ. Desolate territory I once saw only as barren wasteland, I now recognize to be a training ground for spiritual champions. Even during those times when God appears to be absent, He is intently working to develop a generation of people who will transform the world. Has any man or woman of God ever accomplished anything of lasting value without having first traversed wilderness territory? No champion will ever be born apart from adversity, and so a life free of challenges will never progress beyond the realm of wishful thinking.

Whether we enter desolate spiritual territory because of God's leading, by our own poor choices, or due to circumstances beyond our control, our sovereign God intends to use every wilderness season to accomplish awesome things in the lives of the children He loves. If, however, we do not understand the nature of the championship event in which we are participating, we will one day find ourselves immersed in confusion, frantically sinking to the bottom of the pool.

THE PURPOSE OF CHAMPIONS IN THE WILDERNESS

Through the years, I have learned that how we posture our hearts in isolated territory can mark the difference between life and death. I can't begin to explain how much it matters that we understand what God seeks to accomplish in our hearts and that we willingly participate in the growth process. In practice, I have not yet mastered all of the concepts expounded upon in this devotional, but in principle, I now know how to orient myself in God's direction during perplexing seasons.

Perhaps the Christian life is more than you bargained for. Perhaps your struggles are daunting and you feel overwhelmed by it all. Perhaps you think you are powerless to change your circumstances, let alone reign over sin. Welcome to the human race! We are all cut from pretty much the same cloth. Our calling is not to stand proudly in judgment over each other's failures, but to lift one another to new heights in Christ. The purpose of what I've written, therefore, is not to condemn you for where you might currently be, but to challenge you get to where your loving Father wants you to go.

HOW TO USE THIS BOOK

In addition to the main body, each devotional reading contains a quote, a biblical passage, personal questions, an action step, a prayer, and additional scriptural references. I have chosen this format because I believe that the learning process is most effective when truth is reinforced and also practically applied. *Champions in the Wilderness* should lend itself well to both individual and small group settings. Healthy small group discussion adds yet another powerful layer to the learning experience. Our challenge is to go from learning a new concept, to understanding it well, to integrating it into our daily lives. Such a task is not accomplished simply by casual effort.

My goal is to challenge you, the reader, to see things from a perspective that may differ from how you currently view life. Please be open minded but don't just accept my—or anyone else's—word on things; take the time to search truth out for yourself. The Holy Spirit is our primary teacher but I have learned that He will use a wide variety of sources to teach us His ways. As a case in point, I probably would not agree with the theology or lifestyle of some of the authors I quoted but their relevant nuggets of truth enriched the quality of this work.

Exactly how you utilize this book is between you and God. However, I encourage you to approach it not as a book, but as a *season*—a season in which you deliberately pull away from unnecessary distractions to draw nearer to your Creator, to a deeper understanding of His mysterious ways, to a life freshly aligned with His kingdom paradigm. Not only will your life be enriched, but in due time, you will find yourself emerging as an overcomer in the likeness of those champions of old whom we so often admire.

ACKNOWLEDGEMENTS

No words—no matter how eloquent—will suffice to express my appreciation to all of those who have helped us to get this book in print. Due to various limitations, many of these fine people must go unmentioned. Eternity, however, will surely broadcast their names.

However, I will list those whose hands, eyes, and intellects helped to complete this labor of love. Our reviewers, Jeff Ference, Wilbur and Violet Hosler, David Kennard, Elaine Rice, Rose Salazar, and Ted Yohe graciously volunteered their time and energies to keep me pointed in the right direction. Our editors, Jeff Dories, Jason Hutchins, Lynda Logue, and Sean McGaughran all played vital roles in helping me through the more tedious aspects of writing and grammar. Tim Bennett's input as a writing and editorial consultant proved to be invaluable. Also, Nathan Miller did an awesome job of creating a unique cover design.

My name is on this book but nothing ever accomplished through SfMe Ministries would have been possible without our faithful prayer and financial partners, and, of course, our ministry volunteers in general.

Finally, I cannot help but thank my loving wife, Debi, who is always supportive—and honest—as I work out my theology in the midst of our real life experiences.

STAGE ONE
UNDERSTANDING THE NATURE OF YOUR JOURNEY

One sees great things from the valley, only small things from the peak.

–G.K. Chesterton, writer

When anyone hears the word of the kingdom and does not understand it, the evil one comes and snatches away what has been sown in his heart.

MATTHEW 13:19 (NASB)

Life can be horribly confusing—and dark—when we fail to understand God's ways. In this first stage of our journey together, we'll seek an understanding of how God desires to work through a wilderness experience.

CHAPTER ONE
BETWEEN A AND B

To those devoid of imagination a blank place on the map is a useless waste; to others, the most valuable part.
                              -Aldo Leopold, author and environmentalist

---

The LORD said, "I have surely seen the affliction of My people who are in Egypt, and have given heed to their cry because of their taskmasters, for I am aware of their sufferings. So I have come down to deliver them from the power of the Egyptians, and to bring them up from that land to a good and spacious land, to a land flowing with milk and honey, to the place of the Canaanite and the Hittite and the Amorite and the Perizzite and the Hivite and the Jebusite. Now, behold, the cry of the sons of Israel has come to Me; furthermore, I have seen the oppression with which the Egyptians are oppressing them. Therefore, come now, and I will send you to Pharaoh, so that you may bring My people, the sons of Israel, out of Egypt."
EXODUS 3:7-10 (NASB)

"A land flowing with milk and honey"—I like the sound of that! What an awesome thought that the Creator of the Universe would hear our cries, feel our pain, and work to bring His children into a place of overflowing abundance. Whether our salvation came in dramatic fashion, like with the Israelites out of Egypt, or within the quiet, supportive environment of a healthy Christian family, what heartfelt assurance it brings to know that heaven smiles upon us with hope for a better tomorrow.

What we don't expect—or even understand for that matter— is that the road from bondage to the abundant fruitfulness of each person's *promised land* unavoidably snakes through desolate wilderness territory. Why this is exactly, is not readily apparent, for God frequently leads us into places that we would not necessarily choose for ourselves. The classic example, of course, is Moses and the ancient nation of Israel. Deliverance from bondage in Egypt: emotional high! Trapped between Pharaoh's army and the Red Sea: frightening low. The parting of the waters: jubilation! Journey into the wilderness of seemingly never-ending dryness: discouragement and despair.

Such a wilderness experience is not to be compared to visiting a national park, complete with concession stands and policed by park rangers. Essentially, a biblical wilderness involved the territory beyond the immediate reach of a city or village, running the gamut from a forested area to a dry, rocky desert. Consider the following description from *Harper's Bible Dictionary*:

> **wilderness**, *a desolate or deserted area devoid of civilization. One Hebrew word above all others is used for 'wilderness,' or 'desert,' in the OT: midbar, indicating both 'that which is desolate and deserted' and 'that which is beyond,' i.e., beyond the limits of settlement and therefore of government control, perceived by both city dwellers and villagers as being essentially disorderly and dangerous, the home of wild beasts and savage wandering tribes.*[1]

"[D]evoid of civilization . . . the home of wild beasts and savage wandering tribes." Sounds like a great place to picnic. Is there a tour bus? I think I'd prefer the movie!

Let's not forget that it was God who led the people of Israel into the wilderness between Egypt and Canaan, just as He led Jesus into the wilderness to be tempted. Does our Creator have a cruel streak, gleefully watching His naïve children squirm as He herds them into miserable places? Absolutely not! Instead, our sovereign Lord sees well beneath the surface of our lives, grasping the wisdom of using unseen resources from seemingly barren territory to produce abundant fruitfulness.

God seeks to accomplish specific purposes in the wilderness, but in many ways the length and difficulty of our stay depends, at least in part, upon our willingness to learn and to yield. Hundreds of thousands of Israelites wandered aimlessly through the wilderness because they refused to align their hearts with God's design. A people of historic promise forfeited indescribable hope in exchange for a confusing existence. A two-week trek became a forty-year sojourn; a journey to a new life became a walk of death as an entire generation failed to receive the blessing intended for them by God.

Today it is somewhat rare for God to lead His people into a physical wilderness, but from a spiritual perspective, dry, desolate places abound—and with no shortage of "wild beasts" and "savage tribes." One needs only to take a few steps toward moral purity to discover how uncivilized this world can be. The importance of how we respond to such challenges is huge, the long-term state of our hearts being formed as the cumulative product of how we navigate "that which is beyond" our control.

In the face of dry times and savage circumstances, we can easily become hardened, jaded, cynical, and increasingly blind to God's faithful love that surrounds us. If you see little or no good around you, it is entirely likely that you have not been responding well to this season of your life. Our other option—and certainly the preferable one—is to squarely face our wilderness circumstances, viewing them through the eye of faith. Those who do so will soon see that beneath the surface of His apparent abandonment, our heavenly Father is painstakingly working out the details of an often invisible, but amazing plan to bless the children He values so highly.

God does indeed promise to guide us from Point A (bondage) to Point B (fruitful abundance), but rarely does He provide clear details of how long the journey will take, or what we will encounter between those two milestones in our lives. The truly wise person will refuse to surrender to despair, but instead recognize that wilderness seasons do not necessarily indicate God's absence, nor are they intended to be never-ending.

PROBING QUESTIONS

What impressions come to your mind at the thought of a wilderness season?

Would you say that most of your wilderness experiences have hardened you, or purified you?

Have you ever had a wilderness period that proved to be particularly fruitful? What good things came out of that season?

ACTION STEP

If you are not currently dedicating time each day to read the Bible and pray, I encourage you to begin to set aside a specific time each day (in a quiet place) to seek God for yourself.

CLOSING PRAYER

Lord God, I choose to give You the freedom to be the God of my life. Please guide my steps and help me to squarely face my wilderness challenges through the eye of faith. May You use this season of my life to accomplish all that You desire.

FURTHER READING

Psalms 95:6-11; Proverbs 3:1-8; Matthew 4:1-11

CHAPTER TWO
THE WILDERNESS THROUGH THE EYE OF FAITH

God's providence is not blind, but full of eyes.
                    –John Greenleaf Whittier, poet

When Joseph's brothers saw that their father was dead, they said, "It may be that Joseph will hate us and pay us back for all the evil that we did to him." . . . Joseph wept when they spoke to him. His brothers also came and fell down before him and said, "Behold, we are your servants." But Joseph said to them, "Do not fear, for am I in the place of God? As for you, you meant evil against me, but God meant it for good, to bring it about that many people should be kept alive, as they are today. So do not fear; I will provide for you and your little ones." Thus he comforted them and spoke kindly to them.

GENESIS 50:15-21 (ESV)

There is good isolation and there is bad isolation. Good isolation sometimes feels bad. Bad isolation feels worse. How can we distinguish between the two? By looking in the rear view mirror! Only in retrospect can we most effectively discern between what felt bad and what felt worse. This is one of those areas of life in which no simple formula can be found. So much depends upon our response to our circumstances.

At its core, a God-ordained wilderness journey is very different from our human tendency to isolate ourselves when things aren't going well. Joseph's spiritual wilderness experience ended in amazing fashion but only because he trusted God in the face of injustice. Another sort of isolation takes place when we retreat into the narrow world of our own thoughts; where we shun not only human interaction, but the person of God as well. Such self-ordained independence is dangerous territory, for the mind left to its own musings forms a breeding ground for dark, life-stealing thoughts of envy, bitterness, and hatred. In these moments, we need to reach out and connect with a friend, a mature leader, or a counselor. We were created for human interaction; nothing good comes of living in our own narrow world.

Yes, there are times when we need to withdraw from the ceaseless noise, clamor, and worldliness of our surrounding culture. Fasting from food or media, or simply turning aside from unnecessary distractions to pursue God can help retune our spirits to the "radio frequency" in which heaven operates. So powerful are these seasons that it is a wonder we do not take them more often. Yes, they are often quite difficult at the onset, but once we overcome the initial hurdles and tune our hearts to our Savior, discomfort inevitably gives birth to sweetness. Such a season is not just about withdrawing into our own private worlds but about actively seeking our loving Creator.

We are not always (at least initially) willing participants in what can become a healthy wilderness journey. Life brings with it seasons and experiences not of our choosing. Perhaps we've been shunned or rejected. Maybe we've been forced to relocate. We may be plagued with chronic pain or sickness. A new direction in life might mean less time with old friends, while the loss of a loved one or a broken relationship can easily send us into lonely, unfamiliar territory. New adherents to the Christian faith will sometimes find that they have come down from the *mountain of salvation* only to be rejected by friends and family, and that the family of God around them fails to behave like a family in any practical capacity.

Strange as it may seem, there are times when God guides us into the wilderness without our recognizing His hand in the process. Such circumstances can make little sense as we grapple to understand whether our isolation is the work of a sovereign God, wayward humans, or an evil devil. Regardless of how we come to find ourselves in the wilderness, processing our difficulties through a filter of faith is essential.

Joseph went through such an experience. Perhaps his attitude contributed to the situation, but what his brothers did by selling him into slavery was unconscionable. It simply should not have happened. But happen it did; more than once Joseph found himself isolated with little or no support. The young man's response to mistreatment and neglect stands as one of the bright moments in all of Scripture. Joseph never questioned God's faithfulness for apparently failing to act on his behalf, but stood strong in faith and faithful in purity, refusing to allow bitter thoughts to overrun his lonely mind. In the end, it became apparent to all that a sovereign, loving God had used sinful human choices to accomplish a spectacular feat: an outcast Hebrew boy had become the second in command of the most powerful nation on earth!

Joseph was not unique. Abraham, Moses, David, and many others experienced wilderness seasons that they did not choose. But, somehow, each was able to see that beyond selfish human choices, and even demonic schemes, the hand of God was moving to accomplish powerful, unseen purposes. Once again, more than anything else, what distinguishes good isolation from bad isolation is our response. If we respond by trusting God regardless of the actions of others, powerful blessings will follow—and not just for us alone. But if we react with anger, cynicism, and suspicion, our isolation morphs into dark tunnels with mournful endings.

Though a wilderness experience may not entirely be of our choosing, how we process such circumstances falls squarely on our own shoulders. Our sovereign God is able to turn even sinful human choices toward His desired, excellent end. That, my friends, is one of the things that makes Him God!

PROBING QUESTIONS

If you are experiencing a time of isolation, try to identify when it began. Can you identify one or more causes?

What types of attitudes have you displayed in the midst of your difficult circumstances?

Is it possible that you are blind to something powerful God wants to do in your life?

ACTION STEP
If your isolation has become toxic due to dark thinking on your part, ask God to guide you in finding a godly person(s) you can trust. Reach out. Get involved. Make deliberate efforts to build healthy connections with at least one trustworthy person.

CLOSING PRAYER
Lord, help me to understand what is happening in my life, and to see Your sovereign hand at work to bring about a good, desirable end. I want to respond to my circumstances in a way that honors You. Please show me how to avoid allowing dark and bitter thoughts to consume my mind.

FURTHER READING
Genesis 37:1-28, 41:1-44; 1 Peter 2:13-25

CHAPTER THREE
HUNGRY FOR HIS PRESENCE

There is a spiritual hunger in the world today—and it cannot be satisfied by better cars on longer credit terms.
                                        –Adlai E. Stevenson II, politician

---

Then the LORD spoke to Moses, "Depart, go up from here, you and the people whom you have brought up from the land of Egypt, to the land of which I swore to Abraham, Isaac, and Jacob, saying, 'To your descendants I will give it.' I will send an angel before you and I will drive out the Canaanite, the Amorite, the Hittite, the Perizzite, the Hivite and the Jebusite. Go up to a land flowing with milk and honey; for I will not go up in your midst, because you are an obstinate people, and I might destroy you on the way." . . . Then he said to Him, "If Your presence does not go with us, do not lead us up from here."
                                        EXODUS 33:1-3, 15 (NASB)

"Audaciously hungry for God"—that is how I am inclined to describe a man like Moses. Why else would an ordinary man so stubbornly refuse to move forward apart from the presence of Almighty God? And why would God, who had had His fill of the wayward Israelites, change His mind to conform to a man's request? Something was going on beneath the surface of what looked to be a family argument. I can't help but conclude that Moses was hungry for God's presence—and that God wanted him to be hungry!

Having such an intense desire for God's presence may seem to be a rather confusing concept because we are told that God is *omnipresent*, meaning *He is everywhere*. God is indeed all around us, but that doesn't mean that all people experience His presence.

Hear the words of the Apostle Paul as recorded in Acts 17:24-27 (HCSB):

> *"The God who made the world and everything in it—He is Lord of heaven and earth and does not live in shrines made by hands. Neither is He served by human hands, as though He needed anything, since He Himself gives everyone life and breath and all things. From one man He has made every nationality to live over the whole earth and has determined their appointed times and the boundaries of where they live. He did this so they might seek God, and perhaps they might reach out and find Him, though He is not far from each one of us."*

In one sense, God is very near to all of us, but at the same time we can be separated from Him by a vast universe. Understanding this is foundational to the gospel! To be *dead in sin* means *to be spiritually separated from our Creator*—even though we can almost reach out and touch Him.

Under the Old Covenant, most of the people of God knew Him only from a distance. Christ's death on the cross changed everything. In the often-quoted text of the third chapter of John (3:3), Jesus proclaimed that no person can see the kingdom of God without being "born again" (or born from above).

When an individual enters into a New Covenant relationship with God, the Holy Spirit enters that person's heart and becomes one with his/her spirit, bringing it to life. I refer to a oneness far exceeding any level of human intimacy. Ponder the thought for a minute. How amazing it is to know and experience the *indwelling* presence of the Creator of the Universe! That He would choose to dwell in the hearts of imperfect, sin-prone humans is one of the great mysteries of all time.

I cannot imagine that God would want to dwell in our hearts without also desiring to make His presence known to us. It is through the *manifestation* of God's presence that He somehow becomes tangible to us, enabling us to sense His nearness. This type of manifestation of God's presence is similar to what Moses sought. It wasn't enough for him to know that God was everywhere around him. Moses wanted to know and experience His nearness—and God wanted him to—as is evidenced by His response.

The manifestation of God's presence in the life of a believer is not automatic. A person consumed with the possessions and activities of this world will see no need to pull to the shoulder of the highway of life in an effort to draw near to his or her Savior. And be mindful that we can grieve and quench His presence by treating others with contempt, wallowing in unbelief, and pursuing various avenues of ungodly living (see Ephesians 4:30-32 and 1 Thessalonians 5:15-22).

As a Christian, I am ever so thankful that God's presence dwells within me, but I am hungry for more. I know that He is always with me, but I want to be with Him, living according to His ways and allowing Him to manifest Himself in increasing measures. No high can compare to tasting the sweetness of the One who designed us!

Those who hunger and thirst for God will be filled. And as the soul's hunger is satisfied through our Lord's presence, the previously indispensable things of this earth begin to lose their draw. Those who feast upon filet mignon have little appetite for greasy hot dogs. In the same way, those who delight in the presence of God will begin to lose their appetite for the unsatisfying menu offered by this present world.

The person who walks with God understands that the solitude of the wilderness can have a refreshing quality. As distractions fade away, we are better able to train our attention to seek His face. May we never despise quiet or obscure seasons, for in the quiet solitude of the wilderness our Savior dwells. I don't know about you, but I want to know and experience more of my Creator!

PROBING QUESTIONS

Why must a person be born again (born from above) in order for God's Spirit to dwell within his or her heart?

What is the difference between God's *indwelling* presence and the *manifestation* of His presence?

According to Ephesians 4:30-32 and 1 Thessalonians 5:15-22, what are some of the things that can hinder us from experiencing God's manifest presence?

ACTION STEP

Take some time to search your heart to see if there might be anything hindering you from drawing near to the God who loves you and wants to be with you.

CLOSING PRAYER

Heavenly Father, I know in my heart that I was not born for this world and that it will never fully satisfy me. Please show me anything that may be keeping us apart. I ask that You reveal Yourself to me. Like Moses, I do not want to go anywhere without You!

FURTHER READING

John 3:1-8, 20:19-22; Acts 2:1-41, 4:23-31

CHAPTER FOUR
THE BREAD OF LIFE

Two things only the people anxiously desire: bread, and the circus games.

—Juvenal, first-century poet

You shall remember all the way which the LORD your God has led you in the wilderness these forty years, that He might humble you, testing you, to know what was in your heart, whether you would keep His commandments or not. He humbled you and let you be hungry, and fed you with manna which you did not know, nor did your fathers know, that He might make you understand that man does not live by bread alone, but man lives by everything that proceeds out of the mouth of the LORD.

DEUTERONOMY 8:2-3 (NASB)

Jesus lived like He was from another world. Having been led by the Holy Spirit into the wilderness, He did not eat for forty days. Forty days—almost six entire weeks! Still, Jesus was God, so we tend to write off His actions as beyond the scope of human ability. But what was Christ's response when tempted by the devil? Notice that Jesus didn't say, "*I* do not live by bread alone." Instead, He proclaimed, "*Man* shall not live on bread alone, but on every word that comes from the mouth of God" (Matthew 4:4).

Do you see it? Those far-off words are not so distant after all; they apply to each of us, including women, because here "man" is used in a generic sense. Christ's wilderness time was never intended to be unique to Him as an individual, but to provide a reflection for all who seek to know God.

It is reasonable to say that the human race is universally preoccupied with food; our existence revolves around breakfast, lunch, and dinner—with snacks in between. Those who struggle with eating disorders are not the only ones who find their minds consumed with thoughts of food. We need food to survive, so it makes perfect sense that its procurement would be at the top of our priority list. We all know, however, that our love affair with the palate goes well beyond simple survival. Whether we speak of bread in the form of pizza, or bread in the form of rice, or bread in the form of pasta, our appetites rule the day. In my younger days, I supposed that sexual lust was the most significant temptation faced by men, but I now realize that the struggle to keep food in its rightful place presents a greater lifelong challenge for both men and women. Even after the twinkle in a man's eye fades, the rumble in his belly will continue to sound.

Our collective struggle with food began when Adam and Eve chose to eat from the tree of the knowledge of good and evil, rather than rely on the life-giving words of God in the garden of Eden. The fruit of that tree looked so good and desirable, and yet it turned to gravel in their mouths. Only after it was too late did our ancient parents understand that our very lives are wrapped up in all that God speaks.

Another form of bread has risen to the top of our priority list in recent years—the bread of entertainment. Life, it seems, can now be found on a screen in a way that makes all else appear dull and worthless. Ah, what more fulfilling time can we have than to watch our favorite sporting event (or movie) while eating an array of mouth-watering foods? Now that's living! Or so we think. Our appetite for food promises much, but delivers little. Entertainment, we might say, delivers even less; we're often quite miserable between shows. Some modern forms of entertainment are less than worthless. Others may have recreational value, but can never begin to serve as a primary form of sustenance.

For many Christians, the danger lies in allowing that which appears to them as *good* to become the enemy of that which is *best*. One of the greatest detriments of a prosperous society is the vast array of distracting opportunities. Each voice clamors for our attention, promising to bountifully feed our souls. Material prosperity—and even Christian activity—matter little apart from a vital relationship with God. Only those who actively seek the best for their lives will grasp that our greatest enemy can be mere good.

A primary problem, it seems, is not with any deficiency on the part of God's provision, but with our lack of effort in pursuing true sustenance. In order to access the true and often inexplicable life of God, we must learn how to move beyond the rumblings of our flesh. Yet, make a decision not to watch your favorite television show, and you will feel your very soul cry out in agony. The same applies to our favorite sports teams, social networking sites, and smart phones. And, if for some reason you would like to multiply the misery, skip lunch or dinner in the process. Attempt to sneak off in prayer and your appetites will undoubtedly follow, nipping at your heels with every step you take.

What life and vitality we miss when we fail to feast upon the true *Bread of Life*! When we turn aside to draw upon God's words, a mysterious strength begins to rise in our souls. Further still, fasting serves as one of the most powerful disciplines ever practiced by followers of Christ.[2] Defying all human logic, heaviness gives way to lightness, anxiety to peace, discouragement to hope. Make no mistake about it, our spiritual provision from heaven bursts with transformational power!

I would like to provide you with a secret formula that enables you to overcome fleshly appetites so that you may soar—the way spiritual giants do—to new heights in God. Unfortunately, I cannot. Really, only two factors come into play. First, do we believe what Jesus spoke in the face of extreme temptation—that "man shall not live on bread alone, but on every word that comes from the mouth of God"? Second, does our hunger for God exceed the natural appetites of our human flesh?

Regardless of why it was initiated (or prolonged), every wilderness experience is intended to demonstrate that our lives hang on every word that proceeds from our Creator's mouth. Grasping this one truth alone has the potential to change the course of our entire lives!

PROBING QUESTIONS

Why is our natural lust for food so powerful?

What can you say about the source of our never-ending desire to be entertained?

Why is it so important for every one of us to understand the reality of "Man shall not live by bread alone, but by every word that proceeds from the mouth of God"?

ACTION STEP

Read John 6:1-63 and record five significant things that stand out to you.

CLOSING PRAYER

Oh, Lord, please help me to know in my heart of hearts that in You alone is true life found. Help me to pursue true sustenance, and satisfy, I pray, the deep hunger of my soul.

FURTHER READING

Psalms 107:1-9; Matthew 4:1-4; John 6:1-63

CHAPTER FIVE
LAND OF THE GIANTS

*David was the last one we would have chosen to fight the giant,
but he was chosen of God.*

–D.L. Moody, evangelist

**Then Caleb quieted the people before Moses and said,
"We should by all means go up and take possession of it, for
we will surely overcome it." But the men who had gone up
with him said, "We are not able to go up against the people,
for they are too strong for us." So they gave out to the sons
of Israel a bad report of the land which they had spied out,
saying, "The land through which we have gone, in spying it
out, is a land that devours its inhabitants; and all the people
whom we saw in it are men of great size. There also we saw
the Nephilim (the sons of Anak are part of the Nephilim);
and we became like grasshoppers in our own sight, and so
we were in their sight."**

NUMBERS 13:30-33 (NASB)

As a kid, I enjoyed watching a television show called *Land of the
Giants* in which a spaceship from Earth crashed on a planet inhabited
by people twelve-times the size of humans. Had the Israelites coming
out of Egypt been able to tune in, they might have kept the show
running longer than just a couple of seasons!

When the people of Israel looked upon those monstrous men
who controlled the territory of the Promised Land, they felt like
little insects crawling through the grass. As a result, a two-week

trek through the wilderness dragged into a forty-year sojourn with an entire generation of Israelites going to their graves before their dreams of the Promised Land could be fulfilled. But it was their own fear of the giants that led to their demise, not the giants themselves.

A very real problem for us is that we tend to profess a depth of faith in God that we do not actually possess. An athletic team may spend a lot of time practicing in preparation for the first game of the season against their arch rivals, but it isn't until they step onto the field of play that their true abilities become evident. Faith is easy on the mountaintop. The battlefield trenches of life are an entirely different matter.

All too often, our version of the gospel speaks only of God's forgiveness in light of our sinfulness, of the efficacy of grace as opposed to our impotent works, of the glories of heaven compared to the pain of this world. All of these things are true, but they fail to present a complete picture. We even go so far as to portray the Old Testament Promised Land as an image of heaven. Do we actually believe that we will have to drive enemies out of heaven? No, each of us has a promised land, a favorable destiny, in this world.

Why is it that every promised land has its share of giants? Why, when we seek that which we believe to be good, must we face health problems, a lack of finances, and all sorts of opposition—not only from others but also from within ourselves? And why, tell me, must these issues loom so large? There are times when a few miniature giants would do me just fine!

We sometimes fail to grasp that God saves us in order to restore us to His image (Romans 8:29), and that His image is that of the ultimate overcomer. God's goal is never to save us for a sweet eternity only, but to transform us into champions of the faith.

By definition, a *champion* is *a person who defeats all opponents*; the more formidable the opposition, the greater the champion. You would be unimpressed if I told you that I once knocked out every kid in my son's fourth-grade class in a boxing tournament. But, if you saw me wearing an Olympic gold medal (that I had actually earned), you would immediately think of greatness. Until we face and overcome genuine giants, we are not true champions in the arena of life.

Our response to our personal giants reveals the true depths of our faith. The fact that we have sufficient faith in one area of life does not necessarily mean that we trust God in all areas. When fear, anxiety, frustration, anger, and bitterness take root in our hearts, they indicate areas in which our faith is shallow. Thus, every giant is, in a sense, *tailor-made* to help us grow in these areas. Am I saying that God is responsible for raising opposition against us? Not necessarily! Our fallen world provides more than enough difficult challenges to our faith. I do know, however, that our loving Father will use even the largest obstacles for His sovereign purposes.

Like the ten doubting spies of Numbers 13, many of us tend to view our giants as signs that God has abandoned us. Very few have the heart of a Joshua or a Caleb. Later in time, only the shepherd boy David stood up against the Philistine champion Goliath, while Saul and all of his mighty men cowered in fear.

How we respond to our giants will impact, not only our lives, but also the generations that follow. Sadly, David had to face Goliath only because Joshua's generation failed to completely destroy their generation of behemoths. We can only imagine how Anak's descendants tormented the nation of Israel for 400 years until a shepherd boy with David's faith happened along. And not only did the kid fell that monster of a man, he used Goliath's own sword to finish the job! God loves to show off by transforming the worst of our weaknesses into our greatest strengths.

The Christian life is played out "from faith to faith" (Romans 1:17). The faith we begin with should never compare to the faith that defines our lives as we near our final breath. That, at least in part, we can attribute to living in the *Land of the Giants*.

PROBING QUESTIONS

Why do we so often feel that God has abandoned us when things are not going well?

If you were to describe your own promised land, how would it look?

What are a couple of giants you are facing right now? In what way might God use them to help you grow strong?

ACTION STEP

Take a few minutes to verbally thank God for the grace that He gives to overcome all difficulties.

CLOSING PRAYER

Father, I thank You that You will never fail or forsake me. Please grant me the grace to courageously face the challenges before me. For Your glory, I want to be a champion of the faith.

FURTHER READING

Numbers 13; 1 Samuel 17:1-53; Romans 1:16-17, 8:28-29

CHAPTER SIX
WHICH WAY DO I GO?

*There are a thousand hacking at the branches of evil to one who
is striking at the root.*

—Henry David Thoreau, author and poet

**The king said to Daniel, whose name was Belteshazzar,
"Are you able to make known to me the dream which I
have seen and its interpretation?" Daniel answered before
the king and said, "As for the mystery about which the king
has inquired, neither wise men, conjurers, magicians nor
diviners are able to declare it to the king. However, there
is a God in heaven who reveals mysteries, and He has
made known to King Nebuchadnezzar what will take place
in the latter days. . . . But as for me, this mystery has not
been revealed to me for any wisdom residing in me more
than in any other living man, but for the purpose of making
the interpretation known to the king, and that you may
understand the thoughts of your mind."**
DANIEL 2:26-30 (NASB)

We named our GPS navigational system "Lady Catherine". Her
title and British accent make us feel dignified and wealthy as we
find our way on a trip. There is a bit of a problem, however. Lady
Catherine is not always correct in her mapping! When traveling in
unfamiliar territory, it is imperative that we have an accurate sense
of the direction in which we should be heading; if we aren't careful,
we may find ourselves driving into someone's front porch! The same

principles apply to a spiritual wilderness. If we have never been to a particular place, losing our way is easy—especially in stormy weather.

I understand that people often refer to the Bible as "a spiritual roadmap for life", but what exactly does that mean? There are times when I feel as though I need a roadmap simply to navigate the pages of the Bible. This creates a significant problem. How can we possibly find our way through a spiritual wilderness, with all of its traps and obstacles, when we have difficulty understanding how to even read our roadmap for life?

Inspired by God through heavenly wisdom, the Bible is not a book that we can figure out with our own human ability—no matter how intelligent we may be. The Creator of the Universe does not live on the same natural plane of existence as humankind. This means that seeking God's wisdom needs to be a top priority for all who desire to see His goodness. When we rant and rave that Christianity doesn't make sense, it is only because we are blind to the dynamic operation of God's benevolent kingdom.

For example, we can only begin to imagine the challenges that Daniel faced as he was jerked from his home and carried into exile to a foreign land. Daniel distinguished himself—even under the threat of death—not due to any measure of personal intelligence, but because of his humble, persistent pursuit of God's wisdom. The results were far reaching. Through the midst of his pain, an entire nation of exiles found hope.

The pursuit of wisdom is a lifelong effort. One simply does not learn to read the spiritual roadmap for life through casual effort. In this we find one of the greatest lessons of the wilderness: God's wisdom is true treasure, more valuable than any riches this world could possibly offer. Wisdom serves as our "tree of life" (Proverbs 3:18) in the midst of barren lands; the fruit of her influence reaches into eternity.

Revelation of God's wisdom is essential to the growth process because the bad fruit we see in our lives does not always resemble the root from which it springs. It is sometimes difficult to accept, but many of our current issues are simply the results (fruit) of processing past struggles in an unhealthy manner.

Let us suppose that I have a problem with anger and lose my temper more often than I care to admit. My focus would be on my bad temper and how to manage it more effectively, yet the root of the issue may go back many years to a dysfunctional childhood. As I fervently seek God's wisdom—giving Him the freedom to serve as my master counselor—He will open my eyes to the root issues involved. I will then be in a position where I can prayerfully process those negative past experiences through the eye of faith, immersed in His faithful love.

As a general rule, it is healthy to have others help us process our ongoing struggles. Whether it be a counselor, a pastor, or a trusted friend, we would do well to open our hearts to those who can provide both loving support and wise counsel. Unfortunately, circumstances do not always provide the luxury of godly counsel, and, ultimately, the input and support of others will have virtually no benefit if we are not personally seeking after God with our entire hearts. This is where a voluntary wilderness experience, such as a personal retreat, can prove invaluable. I have received untold benefit from seasons of fasting and prayer through which I reorient my heart toward God, diligently praying to know Him and His ways.

Do you wrestle with problems that you feel should be behind you? Are there hurts that simply won't go away? Does the path to healing, wholeness, and peace elude you? It may well be worth skipping a meal, or turning off your favorite television show to cry out in prayer for insight and understanding with regard to your circumstances. God's wisdom is our tree of life! Not only will it help us to make sense of the course of our lives, but in its leaves we will find the healing balm of heaven.

PROBING QUESTIONS
What is the problem with trying to figure out the Bible with our own intelligence?

Why is it so important that we humbly seek God if we are to find wisdom?

How can wisdom bring healing to the broken areas of our lives?

ACTION STEP
Grab your calendar and schedule a time when you can skip a meal or a television show to pray for wisdom.

CLOSING PRAYER
Teach me Your ways O, Lord. Open my eyes to Your ways and fill my heart with wisdom.

FURTHER READING
Proverbs 3:1-18, 8; Revelation 22:1-2

CHAPTER SEVEN
ONE STEP AT A TIME

Here on the mountain I have spoken to you clearly: I will not often do so down in Narnia. Here on the mountain, the air is clear and your mind is clear; as you drop down into Narnia, the air will thicken. Take great care that it does not confuse your mind.
                                    –Aslan, *The Chronicles of Narnia:*
                                        The Silver Chair by C.S. Lewis

---

Ahab told Jezebel everything that Elijah had done and how he had killed all the prophets with the sword. So Jezebel sent a messenger to Elijah, saying, "May the gods punish me and do so severely if I don't make your life like the life of one of them by this time tomorrow!"

Then Elijah became afraid and immediately ran for his life. When he came to Beer-sheba that belonged to Judah, he left his servant there, but he went on a day's journey into the wilderness. He sat down under a broom tree and prayed that he might die. He said, "I have had enough! LORD, take my life, for I'm no better than my fathers."
                                        1 KINGS 19:1-4 (HCSB)

Spiritually speaking, the mountaintop is where we would all prefer to live. Nothing in this world can compare to those divine moments of brilliance when the cares and struggles of life fade into oblivion. These are times in drawing near to God when we feel as though we can reach out and touch heaven, times when His voice and calling ring crystal clear, times when we'll do anything He asks regardless of the cost.

I had several mountaintop experiences (and saw many more) during the sixteen plus years that I served as a campus pastor. During that time, we planned and attended dozens of college ministry conferences and retreats with a vision to invest in the coming generations. Every event was life changing to one degree or another as we saw the Holy Spirit powerfully touch young people who had set aside their studies and their work to draw nearer to God.

During that time, I watched a consistent pattern emerge: mountaintop experiences are feel good events usually sandwiched between two bookends of difficulty. Getting to the retreats always proved to be a major challenge as the gates of hell fiercely resisted the advance of God's kingdom; and, coming down off the mountain to return to the "real" world wasn't always pleasant. (Often, we are the most vulnerable to attack as we relish a recent victory.) The voice of God, which seemed clear and obvious only the day prior, could, in an instant, vaporize into the fuzzy mist of a distant dream. It wasn't that the mountaintop experiences were not real; it's just that the visions received on high must be lived out in the trenches of life's valleys.

Of course, we like to think that events are the key to growth. "If we can just get Bob to the conference," we muse, "his life will be radically changed." And often it is—but only when the event is followed by a faithful, daily pursuit of God through the mundane affairs of life. What began at the event can be fully realized only through the *process*. True growth may at times come in leaps and bounds, but in between those leaps and bounds, we must take a series of incremental steps—steps which sometimes stretch for very long distances.

Gazing ahead of us, further into the wilderness, we often wonder how we can do it, how we can possibly endure such a potentially dry and difficult span. The answer is always the same: we advance by God's grace as we take one incremental step at a time. Sometimes they are big strides, sometimes faltering baby steps, but always, they are steps.

We all have times when we feel as though we cannot move forward, not even a fraction, but we fail to realize that even a cry can be a step in the right direction. I remember times of such weakness when all I could do was lie on my couch and cry out to God. But, in crying out to my heavenly Father for help and grace, I was still moving forward regardless of how miserable I felt. Any heartfelt move in God's direction should be considered forward progress.

Somewhere, somehow, we have come to develop the mentality that a "good" Christian never struggles, and, like knights in shining armor, we are to ride forward with ease, entirely free of fear. Struggle, we inherently believe, is a form of weakness not to be seen in the lives of those who truly walk with God. But the Bible tells us that Elijah was a man "with a nature like ours" (James 5:17); his weakness is quite evident. Add to the mix Christ's promises of persecution, and how could we ever begin to think that any of us should be immune to weakness and struggle?

Elijah found himself severely tested as everything inside of him wanted to quit. Still, he took a significant step forward by turning toward God and fully expressing his despair. Through Elijah's humility, even though beset by human weakness—or perhaps because of it—God strengthened him to rise up and continue his journey with supernatural power.

Yes, your wilderness journey may appear to be unending. And, yes, you may feel as though you can't take another faltering step. But you can cry out to God! You can pray through the Psalms, expressing your struggles and your pain. He will be there to meet you with His always-sufficient grace. The greatest failure in life is not to struggle, but to quit. Let's keep moving forward, *One Step at a Time*.

PROBING QUESTIONS

Was there a God-given vision that once burned in your heart but has somehow faded into a distant memory?

Can you recall a time when you were tempted to give up, but found yourself incredibly thankful that you kept on going?

What does the process of moving forward in God look like in your personal life?

ACTION STEP

Revisit a mountaintop experience in which you believed that God spoke to you. Write down your memories of that experience and surrender them to God, giving Him the freedom to order your steps. If you have never had a mountaintop experience with God, ask for one, setting apart an extended time—or attending a Christian retreat—to seek His presence.

CLOSING PRAYER

Lord, thank You so much that You have good plans and purposes for my life! Help me to understand this deep in my heart. Please grant me the grace to continue to pursue You day by day, step by step, regardless of how difficult my life may be.

FURTHER READING

1 Kings 19:1-8; Psalms 102:1-22; Isaiah 54:11-17

CHAPTER EIGHT
HOW LONG, O LORD?

I'll tell you one thing about fruit: you will never see a fruit factory. Isn't that right? You see a shirt factory, but you see a fruit orchard. You see, there is no fruit without life. You cannot manufacture patience.

— Adrian Rogers, pastor and author

Then God said, "Let Us make man in Our image, according to Our likeness; and let them rule over the fish of the sea and over the birds of the sky and over the cattle and over all the earth, and over every creeping thing that creeps on the earth." God created man in His own image, in the image of God He created him; male and female He created them. God blessed them; and God said to them, "Be fruitful and multiply, and fill the earth, and subdue it; and rule over the fish of the sea and over the birds of the sky and over every living thing that moves on the earth."

GENESIS 1:26-28 (NASB)

Our heavenly Father often leads us into territories "beyond civilization" that He might produce true civilization within us. How many men and women of God through the ages have found themselves wandering through desolate territory, all the while wondering how long their season of isolation would last? In part, the question reveals the answer: longer than a person would expect. But how long should such a season last? A wilderness season can serve as a time of preparation to enable the fulfillment of a promise; the end-goal is a supernatural measure of spiritual fruitfulness. Thus, the experience will last as long as it takes for the seed of God's word to fully germinate and produce a fruitful harvest in our hearts.

The concept of spiritual fruitfulness is not new to God's grand design for humanity, but it is new to many of us. Part of the confusion lies in the fact that we tend to limit Genesis 1:26-28 to physical fruitfulness—meaning having lots of kids. But there is a spiritual element to this passage as well. The people of Israel multiplied rapidly in the days of the patriarchs. Even so, severe judgment came upon them because they failed to bear spiritual fruit that honored God (see Isaiah 5:1-7). Let's not deceive ourselves! Fruitfulness always has been, and always will be, integral to God's plan for each and every one of our lives. No exclusions. No exceptions.

Evangelicals tend to think of fruitfulness in terms of sharing their faith and leading others to Christ—and while this is certainly integral to the process, there is more, much more. Biblical fruitfulness involves abiding in a grace-filled relationship with God so that we are conformed to the image of Jesus Christ. As we abide in Christ—the vine—the nine attributes (love, joy, peace, patience, kindness, goodness, faithfulness, gentleness and self-control) of the fruit of the Holy Spirit (Galatians 5:22-23) cannot help but grow in our hearts. In due season, this fruit matures and begins to reproduce itself in the lives of others. We teach what we know. We reproduce who we are. Fruitfulness, at its core, is about reproducing who we have become.

The *Great Commission* (as found in Matthew 28:18-20) given by Jesus was not merely to get people to make some kind of a decision for God; rather, it was a call to "make disciples." Jesus was commanding them (and us) to learn His ways, to be conformed into His image, and to sow into the lives of others what they learned through their own spiritual transformation.

It is not that we are unable to impact others before fully maturing (my life has been touched by people who are no longer even walking with God), but for our lives to reach their full potential, coming to maturity as Spirit-formed representations of Christ is not optional. Gifts, talents, and hard work are critical to the advancement of God's purposes, but they form only a limited part of the equation.

Our Father loves to use zealous people to deeply impact others, but there will be huge problems for the individual whose gifts and talents habitually exceed his or her character. And here's where it gets good: a barren wilderness can be fertile territory where the fruit of the Holy Spirit flourishes!

Through more than thirty years of seeking God, studying the Bible, and watching people, I have concluded that fruitfulness is how God defines success. Sadly, we often ignore any meaningful quest for fruitfulness as we run the all-consuming race for humanly-defined success. We think that if only we can get x number of people to attend our meetings, achieve such and such a status, and have a certain amount of money to accomplish our mission, then God will be pleased. No, this is humankind's definition of success—something vastly different from what God values.

Those who resist being formed into the image of Christ will only multiply the bad fruit in their lives. When gift-oriented success is achieved without genuine fruitfulness, some type of catastrophic collapse will occur—and many lives will be sadly damaged. I could provide you with examples but that would be unnecessary—they've been pasted across the headlines for many years now. Let's not delude ourselves! The fruit of the Holy Spirit explodes into its full measure of multiplication only *after* the wilderness process has been allowed to accomplish its internal purposes.

One of the most effective things we can do during a wilderness season is to pray for the Holy Spirit to illuminate our hearts, enabling us to understand how God desires to use our current season to produce eternal fruit. If we understand what God seeks to accomplish, we can choose to abide in His life-giving grace. This course of action is so much more desirable than sinking into worry, complaining, and hard-heartedness—all expressions of unbelief.

A God-ordained wilderness season will extend until it has given birth to the fruit of the Holy Spirit. We can sometimes limit its duration by fully aligning ourselves with His good plans and purposes, but many a wilderness season has been unnecessarily extended due to ignorance of God's expectations and desires.

God will move in our lives when He is ready to move. It is not something that we can force; our call is to faithfully abide in Him through desolate times. He always has a plan, but in many ways the timing of that plan is dependent upon the seeds that are sprouting beneath the surface of our hearts.

PROBING QUESTIONS

What is the difference between fruitfulness and the world's definition of success?

Why is it essential that we understand how God sees the two differently?

What is spiritual maturity and how is it related to fruitfulness?

ACTION STEP

Take a close look at your life, identifying and recording any areas in which you may be hindering God's efforts to make your life eternally fruitful.

CLOSING PRAYER

Lord, please give me a clearer understanding of Your desire for my fruitfulness, and how it may be practically achieved.

FURTHER READING

Psalms 1; Isaiah 5:1-7; Matthew 28:18-20; Galatians 5:22-23

CHAPTER NINE
NEVER TAKE A WILDERNESS SHORTCUT!

God can never entrust His Kingdom to anyone who has not been broken of pride, for pride is the armor of darkness itself.
—Francis Frangipane, pastor and author

A voice is calling,
"Clear the way for the LORD in the wilderness;
Make smooth in the desert a highway for our God.
Let every valley be lifted up,
And every mountain and hill be made low;
And let the rough ground become a plain,
And the rugged terrain a broad valley;
Then the glory of the LORD will be revealed,
And all flesh will see it together;
For the mouth of the LORD has spoken."

ISAIAH 40:3-5 (NASB)

We humans make for fascinating study! We are so diverse in some ways; so similar in others. There are general stereotypes, however, that do apply to almost all of us—at least to a degree. One such grouping would be the "haves" versus the "have nots"; the "somebodies" versus the "nobodies".

The somebodies might be compared to those in the homecoming court being honored at a high school football game. Almost without fail, the king and queen are attractive, athletic, and immensely popular. Rarely does such public favor suddenly appear, so they generally have been accustomed to being at the top of the popularity ladder. Not always, but often enough, these individuals develop an air of self-confidence—frequently to the point of arrogance.

At the bottom of the popularity ladder we find the nobodies, of which there are two types. The "wallflower nobodies" are the ones who no one really ever notices; like extras filling in the background crowd of a movie, their presence is necessary, but obscure. The wallflower nobodies often look with envy upon the somebodies who always seem to land the key roles, quietly wishing that they too could have such a sense of significance.

Even less fortunate than the wallflower nobodies are the "nobody nobodies"—those who serve as the objects of scorn and ridicule for everyone else. I speak of the poor individuals who would welcome the invisibility of their wallflower counterparts, people who often live in a world of dark emotions, overcome by feelings that move beyond envy and into the realm of hatred. Having been publicly humiliated and treated unjustly more times than they can count, their view of life becomes increasingly jaded and bitter.

At first glance, the somebodies and the nobodies appear to be two very different groups of people, but both are driven by self-centered pride. The king and queen will often behave arrogantly because they believe they are favored due to their own inherent greatness. Having become accustomed to the praise of human approval, they don't have a clue how incomplete they actually are. On the other hand, the nobodies can be self-centered in that they come up short in their constant pursuit of self-significance. They are incomplete and they know it. One group is defined by a personal sense of glory and the other by a lack thereof. In the end, both seek glory, but in the eyes of God neither approach is acceptable!

If there is anything that keeps God at a distance, it is human pride in whatever form it takes. God seeks to use wilderness experiences to bring low the arrogance of the somebodies, and to lift up the self-effacing woefulness of the nobodies. Through desert experiences, those who brim with confidence will come to realize the foolish futility of self-trust. Those plagued by a poor self-image, on the other hand, will not learn to find significance in themselves as they naturally wish, but to see their treasured value in the eyes of our loving Father. Another purpose of the wilderness, then, is to expose false foundations of identity with the intention of forging an entirely new sense of what defines us.

Not only does this process run contrary to the world system which surrounds us, it also conflicts with the way the church at large has operated for centuries. Far too many seek a sense of personal significance from their service, their position, their knowledge, or their religious connections (e.g. denomination). And although we may serve in the name of Christ, the cumulative results of our personal pursuits of glory will hinder the advance of God's glorious kingdom. If the church is full of self-centered pride, little hope remains for the world in which we live.

To attempt to take a wilderness shortcut, then, is to oppose God's plan to build a smooth highway through which His glory will be revealed. By seeking an easy way out of the wilderness, we will, in the long-run, hinder that which we profess to establish. Having taken my share of shortcuts in my life (just ask my family), I have learned that there are times when it is wise to stay on the main road—even when the journey feels as though it will never end.

Adam and Eve attempted to take a shortcut by eating from the tree of the knowledge of good and evil. Rather than learning, day by day, through an intimate relationship with their Creator, they sought to bypass the learning process, only to leave themselves—and their descendants—in dire straits. Abram and Sarai also tried a shortcut (see Genesis 16:1-12); we continue to experience the fallout of that one as well, not only in the Middle East, but all over the globe. Jesus, on the other hand, serves as our stellar example. He never sought the easy way out, always entrusting Himself fully to the Father's wise plan.

There was a day when I considered myself to be a nobody nobody. I hated it! Now looking back, however, I understand that my personal lack of self-significance helped me to recognize my desperate need for God. Since coming to Christ, my identity has been painstakingly forged by God, not in the arena of public approval, but in the solitude of the wilderness.

Whether you see yourself as a somebody, or a nobody; whether you feel as though you have something to offer, or you don't; whether you have entered the wilderness because of foolish and prideful decisions, or you have been driven by the cruel oppression of others, God's desire is to use your current situation to help forge an eternal sense of humble significance in your heart. Taking a backcountry shortcut would not be wise as they tend to extend the duration of an undesirable wilderness experience.

PROBING QUESTIONS

How have you traditionally defined yourself—as a "somebody" or a "nobody"? Why?

In what ways are arrogance and self-deprecation both forms of the same destructive pride?

How can the wilderness serve to create a smooth highway for God's glory to be revealed?

ACTION STEP

Write a list of the ways in which you have attempted to find a sense of self-significance apart from God. Surrender these things to the heavenly Father, giving Him complete freedom to transform your identity.

CLOSING PRAYER

Lord God, I fully surrender my sense of identity to You and ask that You reshape my self-image according to Your excellent and eternal design. With all my heart, I want to see Your glory revealed!

FURTHER READING

Genesis 3:1-8, 16:1-12; 1 Corinthians 12:12-27; Galatians 3:23-29

CHAPTER TEN
THE END OF YOUR SELF

Do you wish to be great? Then begin by being. Do you desire to construct a vast and lofty fabric? Think first about the foundations of humility. The higher your structure is to be, the deeper must be its foundation.

— Augustine, church father

"Moses fled and became an exile in the land of Midian, where he fathered two sons. After 40 years had passed, an angel appeared to him in the wilderness of Mount Sinai, in the flame of a burning bush."

ACTS 7:29-30 (HCSB)

It was one of the most painful moments of my Christian life. I had been walking with God for about five years and felt a strong call to "full-time" ministry. At that point, my world was small as I thought my only two options were to pastor a church, or ship off to a tropical mission field. I really like ice in my drinks (not to mention hot showers)[3], so I decided that pastoring was the call for me. Plans were made and the appropriate steps taken, but the door slammed shut! My wife, Debi, and I had planned to visit a seminary only to find that her boss would not allow her to take the time off work.

There are times in life when God redirects our steps, and there are times when we need to press through the obstacles that stand in our way. Not understanding the difference, I tried to force the issue, precipitating what became an epic marital "discussion". I could not accept the idea of not heading toward ministry training; my entire identity was wrapped up in becoming a successful pastor.

There we were, Debi and I, in bed, with our backs turned against each other and our hearts filled with anger and frustration. Neither of us was willing to budge. An ominous darkness filled my mind as I began to realize that my ministry calling would not be fulfilled any time soon. (My thoughts were accurate—what I had hoped would be a short season gradually stretched into a seventeen-year wilderness experience that lasted until I was able to enter campus ministry as a vocation.)

I wish I could say that if you picked up book *XYZ* and read paragraph three on page twelve, you would find the formula to distinguish when to let go and when to press through. No such formula exists. However, I did come to understand a spiritual principle closely mirroring the natural world: in order to effectively and safely *build up*, one must first *dig down* to lay a rock-solid foundation. Otherwise, a collapse is inevitable. Even when building on a warm, sunny day, the wise builder never cuts corners, always preparing for the violent storms that will assuredly blow some distant day.

It seems almost bizarre to be digging in the opposite direction of the one we seek to build. But if we desire to build to the heights, we must first dig to the depths. And the lower we go, the more difficult the process becomes; the ground becomes harder, and rocks—sometimes very large ones—block our way. Digging often slows to a snail's pace, revealing little progress in spite of all of the effort invested. And, probably worst of all, the deeper the foundation sinks, the darker the environment becomes. As the light begins to fade, as the world appears to grow dim, as we feel that all of our dedication and hard work have amounted to little, our self-confidence begins to waver, piercing the ego like an arrow through the heart.

From all outward appearances, framing a building is the antithesis of laying a strong foundation. Erecting walls is fast and progress readily visible. After a day of framing, a crew can look at their work with satisfaction, relishing what they have been able to accomplish in only a short period of time. And so we build upward, with dreams of reaching to the skies for the glory of God (or so we tell ourselves). But a house without a secure foundation is a disaster waiting for an opportunity. It is not a matter of *if* the storms will come, but *when*. Always build for the storm!

For several years, our family vacationed along the coast of North Carolina. Our hearts would leap with excitement as we arrived at the shore and drove toward our rental condo. Like country bumpkins on their first visit to the city, we would gawk and admire all of the expensive houses along the coast. One especially beautiful home always stood out as we fantasized about what it would be like to own— that is until a couple of hurricanes ravaged the North Carolina coast. Upon returning the following summer, our jaws dropped as we gazed upon that once beautiful vacation home now marred by a huge split right down the middle. Beyond repair, it would soon be demolished. That expensive house, once the envy of all, had become the object of gawkers because its foundation proved to be insufficient for the scope and intensity of the storm.

Somehow, we have managed to convince ourselves that a healthy foundation consists entirely of head knowledge. In doing so, we fail to grasp that obedient faith and godly character are firmly established only as we come face to face, through the light of God's love, with our own *inabilities*. What better place to discover our limitations—and to lay a firm foundation—than in a spiritual wilderness? Would Moses have been able to deliver the people of Israel had he not spent forty years living with his failure in the wilderness? Only God knows for sure.

Some of us can run far and jump high, relying on our own strengths and abilities, accomplishing a great deal along the way. Still, the day will come when the clouds grow dark, the winds blow, and the rain falls. At that point, strength of self will be of no value, and the opportunity to construct a secure foundation will have passed. Now is the time to prepare your foundation, to build for the storm—its winds will one day blow much harder than anyone expects. Never despise the days of obscure, but faithful obedience as you navigate the wilderness territory before you. They are helping to create strength of character that you will desperately need further down the road of life.

PROBING QUESTIONS

What does it mean to build a strong spiritual foundation?

What are some of the dangers involved with trying to build up without first digging down?

How can God use a wilderness season to help lay a rock-solid foundation in our lives?

ACTION STEP

List all of the reasons you can to explain why we are often tempted to cut corners in the building process.

CLOSING PRAYER

Holy Spirit, please search my heart and show me if my spiritual foundation is lacking in any way. I want to be rock-solid in You!

FURTHER READING

Exodus 2:11-25, Psalms 139; Matthew 7:24-27

CHAPTER ELEVEN
THE STILL, SMALL VOICE OF GOD

Prayer is not monologue, but dialogue. God's voice in response to mine is the most essential part.

—Andrew Murray, pastor and author

So He said, "Go forth and stand on the mountain before the LORD." And behold, the LORD was passing by! And a great and strong wind was rending the mountains and breaking in pieces the rocks before the LORD; but the LORD was not in the wind. And after the wind an earthquake, but the LORD was not in the earthquake. After the earthquake a fire, but the LORD was not in the fire; and after the fire a sound of a gentle blowing. When Elijah heard it, he wrapped his face in his mantle and went out and stood in the entrance of the cave. And behold, a voice came to him and said, "What are you doing here, Elijah?"

1 KINGS 19:11-13 (NASB)

We walk in the house; on goes the TV. We close the car door; on goes the radio. We sit on the park bench; up comes the smart phone. Like couch potatoes stuffing our mouths with junk food, so we fill our ears with noise, noise, noise. Of course, it is not just any noise—sometimes we're very particular about what we listen to. Whether pleasant or obnoxious, quiet or loud, wanted or unwanted, all of our background noise has the cumulative effect of drowning out *The Still, Small Voice of God* (1 Kings 19:12).

Ironically, one of the most asked questions by Christians is how to hear the voice of God. And yet, by our very actions, we crowd out our Father's efforts to speak to His beloved children. Why do we do this? Perhaps we don't understand how He speaks. Maybe it's because we don't like some of the things we hear—or think we hear—Him saying. Sadly, some Christians don't even believe that God speaks to His children apart from the Bible. That doesn't sound like much of a relationship to me!

Confusion can sometimes abound as we try to delineate between God's voice and our own human thoughts. Many of us can't bear what surfaces in our hearts and minds when the world grows quiet. Much better not to go there! All too frequently, we mistake the voice of conscience for the voice of God. The conscience, which is motivated by law, speaks more loudly, more often, and with a relentless force of condemnation that leaves us feeling beat up and miserable. Equating the voice of conscience with God's voice paints a negative image of God in our hearts, leaving us hesitant—or even afraid—to hear what He has to say.

The Holy Spirit, who is always motivated by love, can communicate with us through a variety of means: through the Scriptures, by using circumstances, via other people, or directly to our hearts and minds. On a very rare occasion, our Lord will speak to His children in an audible voice. At other times, clear sentences mystically enter our minds. Most often, it seems that God speaks to our regenerated spirits through impressions in the heart; the subtle nature of which require listening ears.

Like the little boy ignoring his mother's call for bedtime, we can easily master the art of avoiding God's quiet call. All we need to do is focus our attention on a convenient distraction, or harden our hearts just a bit. The time will soon come when all sensitivity to the quiet voice is lost and we are free to follow our own paths—and to be entrapped by our own devices.

The combination of these and other factors will lead us to a narrow, hopeless place. While the quiet voice of God is the only effective answer to our ills, we often extend the length and intensity of our wilderness experiences because we fail to take the time to listen. But how can we listen when silence equals pain or confusion?

Faith in God is the answer! Elijah ran to God and not away from Him. Although in deep pain and despair of soul, Elijah believed his future to be safe and bright in his heavenly Father's capable hands. He could tune in to the voice of heaven's gentle breeze because he was confident it would carry a message of hope, not one of condemnation. Even living under the strict standards of the Mosaic Law, Elijah understood the kind, merciful nature of our heavenly Father.

The Bible plays a critical role in our learning to hear the quiet voice of God. It is through the Scriptures that we discover how to tune our spiritual receivers to His frequency. We also need an objective framework through which we can process our subjective thoughts. Apart from the unchanging truths of God's written word, we are more likely to entertain dangerous and deceptive voices that our minds should otherwise silence. During all seasons of life, but especially wilderness times, the Bible serves as an indispensable guide to the heart of God.

Let us not fail, however, to realize that what we read in the Scriptures must be processed by faith in light of the New Covenant of grace. Far too often, we mistakenly view the teachings of the New Testament through the lens of Old Testament law. The Bible, then, becomes a book of rules to obey. Make no mistake about it: evil voices will use every opportunity—including Bible reading—to overwhelm our hearts and minds with the weight of condemnation. The unfortunate result is that we then find ourselves hesitant to immerse ourselves in the one book with the potential to transform our circumstances, freeing us from our burdens of guilt and shame.

When we come to the end of self, condemnation is the last thing needed, and thankfully, it is the last thing our loving Savior would heap onto our shoulders. If we hear the familiar ring of a condemning voice, we can rest assured that it is not the sound of our Savior speaking. The conviction of the Holy Spirit may hurt for a short while, but it always carries with it a sense of hope for the future. May we learn to block out the voices that are loud, distracting, and condemning as we tune our hearts to the quiet call of our loving Lord. His every word drips with true and lasting life!

PROBING QUESTIONS

Do you believe that God desires to speak to you? Why or why not?

Why is the Bible essential to learning to hear God's voice?

What is it that sometimes makes us feel condemned when we read the Bible?

ACTION STEP

If you are not doing so already, begin to take periods of time in which you shut off the noise and read the Bible. (Some information about translations can be found at the beginning of Appendix I). Start small if needed, deliberately laying hold of His promises and casting down all condemning thoughts.

CLOSING PRAYER

Oh Lord, please teach me to hear Your voice, for Your words are my life.

FURTHER READING

John 10:1-16; Romans 8:1-4; 2 Corinthians 3:1-6

CHAPTER TWELVE
INHERITANCE OF HOPE

Give me the love that leads the way,
The faith that nothing can dismay
The hope no disappointments tire,
The passion that will burn like fire;
Let me not sink to be a clod;
Make me Thy fuel, Flame of God

—Amy Carmichael, missionary to India

Blessed be the God and Father of our Lord Jesus Christ, who according to His great mercy has caused us to be born again to a living hope through the resurrection of Jesus Christ from the dead, to obtain an inheritance which is imperishable and undefiled and will not fade away, reserved in heaven for you, who are protected by the power of God through faith for a salvation ready to be revealed in the last time.

1 PETER 1:3-5 (NASB)

Imagine that you have been lost in the wilderness for several days. You're suffering from exposure and are famished for lack of provision. Eating bugs simply isn't cutting it, which is unfortunate because every insect within miles has taken nest in your hair and clothes. Slowly and painfully you trudge up a rocky hillside in search of a better vantage point, and as you finally peer over the brim of the hill, your suddenly attentive gaze settles upon the prettiest little community ever to capture your eyes.

What happens in your heart at this moment? Do you drop to your knees in despair? Do you weep in desperate agony? Do fear and anxiety fill your heart? No, no, and no! Immediately your heart comes alive! A new sense of strength enters your bones. Even with the difficult journey remaining, you envision friendly people welcoming you into their homes for a hot bath and a warm, delicious meal.

Early in youth, we are often full of hopefulness—we have not yet experienced enough of life's pains and disappointments to steal our optimism. Some of us haven't carried the full weight of never-ending burdens. We haven't felt the betrayal of trust by those who should be worthy of our confidence. We haven't yet grasped the degree to which selfishness and cruelty color this planet. As such worldly realities become more and more real to us, a vague sense of futility may begin to cloud our vision; a feeling of hopelessness can sink into our hearts. This is a fallen world replete with human brokenness. We cannot help but experience difficulty—and even injustice—during our days on earth.

There are times when this entire world seems like a barren, unfriendly wilderness; days when all the news is bad and virtually every area of life seems difficult and unpleasant. All too often, difficult days extend into painful seasons as weariness and discouragement take root in our souls. "Why even bother to try to do good?" is a question we might find ourselves asking. If discouragement is our goal, opportunity abounds.

A particular effect of an unwelcomed wilderness experience is that a survey of our surrounding landscape can produce a disheartening sense of hopelessness. No matter what direction we travel, and regardless of how far, the natural eye convinces us that the distance is too great; therefore, every imaginable path becomes dark and foreboding. Still, much of our negativity is mostly a matter of perception.

Hope can be defined as *the desire for something good, with an underlying expectation that good will be received or achieved.* Our world is full of false hope, but biblical hope is more than some vague belief. Built upon the reality of Christ, hope will carry us through our most difficult seasons.

I don't think we understand much about our eternal inheritance in Christ. Most often we think of heaven, which feels far off and nebulous. We remember hearing something about mansions and streets of gold, but it is difficult to envision a place we have never seen. Like first-time parents trying to imagine how their baby will look, we can't grasp the picture of an eternal inheritance.

We do, however, find a powerful clue in Paul's letter to the Ephesians:

> *In Him, you also, after listening to the message of truth, the gospel of your salvation—having also believed, you were sealed in Him with the Holy Spirit of promise, who is given as a pledge of our inheritance, with a view to the redemption of God's own possession, to the praise of His glory.* Ephesians 1:13-14 (NASB)

A *pledge* in this sense is *a down payment given to provide an assurance of something greater to come.* Do you see it? The Holy Spirit is the down payment of our inheritance in Christ! Our promised land is defined by a promised *Person*—the Holy Spirit. If God Himself is the down payment, what must the inheritance be? We can only imagine.

I love that Peter writes of the "living hope" we have in Christ. Hope is not something we normally envision as being alive. Regardless of whether we have entered a wilderness season willingly in pursuit of God, or if circumstances beyond our control have left us feeling isolated and weary, we can expect a glorious inheritance from God because the Holy Spirit is with us wherever we go. No matter how low we may sink, or what confusion clouds our thinking, the full potential of heaven dwells within us through the person of the Holy Spirit! The secret of hope, then, involves giving Him the freedom to reign as God in our daily lives.

Once again, we must ask, "How are we to respond to a wilderness environment?" Do we walk in integrity, seeking to glorify our Savior through all of our words and actions? Do we forgive freely? Do we treat others with honor and respect regardless of their perceived worthiness? Do we rivet our hope on that which is eternal and imperishable? It is a real hope that we need—one that never fails to provide strength in the midst of barren desert territory.

Not only is the hope that He provides unquenchable, it brings life to our weary hearts. In all honesty, I cannot even begin to understand the full extent of our hope in Christ. But as I peer over the crest of the hill and into the glory of God's nearness, my heart jumps with excitement. When illuminated by our living hope, a gray, dismal wilderness suddenly shines with an eternal glory!

PROBING QUESTIONS
What does hope mean to you?

Is there an area of your life where hopelessness has fastened its grip?

How does the Holy Spirit make our hope a *living* hope?

ACTION STEP
List five things about our inheritance in Christ that bring life and anticipation to your soul.

CLOSING PRAYER
Jesus, thank You for Your living hope that destroys all darkness and despair. Please open my eyes that I may grasp all that hope entails.

FURTHER READING
Isaiah 40:27-31; Romans 5:1-5; Ephesians 1:15-23

CHAPTER THIRTEEN
SPRINGS IN THE DESERT

No difficulties in your case can baffle him, no dwarfing of your growth in years that are past, no apparent dryness of your inward springs of life, no crookedness or deformity in any of your past development, can in the least mar the perfect work that he will accomplish, if you will only put yourselves absolutely into his hands and let him have his own way with you.

–Hannah Whitall Smith, speaker and author

Thus says the LORD:
"Cursed is the man who trusts in man
and makes flesh his strength,
whose heart turns away from the LORD.
He is like a shrub in the desert,
and shall not see any good come.
He shall dwell in the parched places of the wilderness,
in an uninhabited salt land.
Blessed is the man who trusts in the LORD,
whose trust is the LORD.
He is like a tree planted by water,
that sends out its roots by the stream,
and does not fear when heat comes,
for its leaves remain green,
and is not anxious in the year of drought,
for it does not cease to bear fruit."

JEREMIAH 17:5-8 (ESV)

Whether the result of greenhouse gases, or due simply to the natural cycles of the Earth and Sun, climate change is a reality. The frequency and intensity of tornadoes in the U.S., for example, has increased dramatically in recent years. Another painful climatological problem is drought—large areas of our world are suffering due to a shortage of rain followed by the loss of valuable crops. Drought-induced famine takes a massive toll on both human and animal life through starvation and its accompanying diseases. Water is, without question, a precious commodity in our world.

It should be no surprise then that *water* is one of the metaphors used in the Scriptures to help illuminate the presence and work of the Holy Spirit. In both the physical and spiritual realms, water represents the essence of our existence. And, as it is with water, the presence of the Holy Spirit is always associated with life. Where His presence is lacking, spiritual famine ensues.

I am not sure how we arrive at such conclusions, but it is common for Christians to believe that God leads them into spiritually dry seasons. As subtle as the difference may seem, we would do well to make a distinction between travelling through a dry environment, and being dry within our hearts. Just as God led the nation of Israel through the desert, so He will sometimes guide His children through dry, desolate places. But the Bible is absolutely clear: He never wants us to be dry in our hearts! If we are spiritually parched, He is not to blame. The only wise option is to take personal ownership of the issue rather than blaming it on the mystical work of a sovereign God.

We must wonder, then, what causes our spirits to wilt with barren dryness. In most (if not all) cases, the culprit is misplaced trust—a reality much more dangerous than it sounds. *Idolatry*—a spiritual condition detestable to God—amounts to *putting someone (or something) other than God on the throne of our hearts*, either as an act of adoration, or in trust as the source of our provision. Because God is invisible, and idols physically tangible, we are tempted to look to idols to meet our physical, emotional, and spiritual needs.

For seventeen years, I worked in the laboratory of the Rochester and Pittsburgh Coal Company (R&P). At first, things were great as the company prospered—even making the Fortune 500 list one year. Unfavorable economic changes, however, led to a long string of layoffs, culminating with the sale and closing of the company. For almost a decade, my coworkers and I lived under the burden of economic uncertainty, watching others lose their jobs and finding ourselves anxious about our own futures. To put it bluntly: in spite of a decent salary, it was a miserable ten years to be working for R&P.

During that particular wilderness season, I discovered that I had a choice. I could attempt to put my trust in the very human managers of the R&P Coal Company, or I could focus on my heavenly Father as the source of my provision. Yes, God was able to use my company to provide for my family, but He wasn't limited to do so. If the provision from R&P was to dry up, He would be sure to lead us to another financial stream to care for our needs.

Subsequently, I chose to move from a full-time to a part-time basis (thereby losing my benefits and taking a big pay cut) to pursue a poorly paying career in college ministry. When the company finally closed its doors two years later, I launched into a career of Christian ministry without ever filing for unemployment. Provision came through a variety of sources, but we never found ourselves in a position where we couldn't pay our bills.

Many of us struggle to keep God as the focus of our trust during times of economic uncertainty, but idolatry isn't limited to just money. We can attempt to put other people in the place of God, expecting them to love us in a way that only He can. Many a romantic relationship has ended within months because an individual in search of a god discovered only a human instead. Another huge (and common) error is to look to various forms of media rather than to the Scriptures to feed our souls; the result being a dysfunctional and unsatisfying addiction to entertainment.

Yes, God may indeed lead us through dry environments, but if we are dry in our souls, the problem is ours and not His. Someway, somehow, we are placing the bulk of our trust in someone or something humanly tangible. Those who attempt to satisfy their spiritual thirst through idolatrous means will undoubtedly poison their spirits with polluted waters full of invisible toxins.

May we fully grasp the truth of our Father's promise: the hearts of those who cultivate faith toward Him will always be well-watered gardens, overflowing with abundant life. How deep is His love that He would teach us to draw upon a never-ending flow of pure, living water!

PROBING QUESTIONS

What stands out to you personally about the contrast identified in Jeremiah 17:5-8?

What is idolatry and why is it so deadly?

Can you think of an area or two in your life where you might be putting the primary weight of your trust in someone or something other than God?

ACTION STEP

If you have been able to identify any areas where your trust is wrongly focused, write out a plan to help redirect your focus.

CLOSING PRAYER

Father, please forgive any misplaced trust or idolatrous tendencies in my life. I desire to honor You above all as my one true source of life and provision. Please help me to do so—I want my life to be a well-watered garden, overflowing with Your Presence!

FURTHER READING

Isaiah 43:16-21, 58:6-12; John 4:7-26, 7:37-39

STAGE TWO
THE WILDERNESS FAITH WALK

Every tomorrow has two handles. We can take hold of it by the handle of anxiety, or by the handle of faith.
—Henry Ward Beecher, pastor and author

The fundamental fact of existence is that this trust in God, this faith, is the firm foundation under everything that makes life worth living. It's our handle on what we can't see. The act of faith is what distinguished our ancestors, set them above the crowd.
HEBREWS 11:1-2 (MESSAGE)

Necessary—and favorable—changes begin to take place as we understand the importance of faith in God and make corresponding adjustments in our lives. Stage Two is intended to help grow a living and vital faith.

CHAPTER FORTEEN
TIME TO SWITCH CAREERS

Faith does not grasp a doctrine, but a heart. The trust which Christ requires is the bond that unites souls with Him; and the very life of it is entire committal of myself to Him in all my relations and for all my needs, and absolute utter confidence in Him as all sufficient for everything that I can require.

–Alexander MacLaren, pastor

And he [Abram] believed in (trusted in, relied on, remained steadfast to) the Lord, and He counted it to him as righteousness (right standing with God).

GENESIS 15:6 (AMP)

For whatever reason, Christians often believe *blessing* and *difficulty* to be mutually exclusive words. Unlike peanut butter and chocolate, blessing and difficulty don't appear to be palatable traveling companions.

When God blesses our lives, shouldn't our circumstances work out with ease? Shouldn't others like and respect us? Shouldn't we prosper in every aspect of our jobs? (Shouldn't we all have jobs?) Shouldn't our ministry efforts go smoothly? After all, God certainly has the ability to make things happen, why wouldn't He—all the time? Shouldn't the Christian life be much easier than it is?

Most would concur that the Apostle Paul lived a blessed life. But when we survey the actual details of Paul's writings, we realize he experienced difficulties for Christ that would make a Navy SEAL wince. Most of his traveling companions abandoned Paul at the end of his life, and yet he was blessed! Without minimizing the importance of provision for physical needs, we would do well to firmly grasp the idea that God's primary blessings are spiritual in nature; it is a feat that can be accomplished only through the eye of faith.

Faith has more to do with God's faithfulness than with our ability to trust; the only reason we are able to believe is because the King of the Universe is absolutely faithful to His word. One of the keys to this process of believing involves learning to recognize the real nature of God rather than falling prey to the ongoing smear campaign first initiated by the serpent in the garden of Eden.

Even though faith is primarily about God's faithfulness, our measure of belief still matters a great deal to our Creator. Faith was the primary attribute by which Jesus identified people. You don't read of the Son of God saying, "O, you plump in figure," or "I have never seen such beautiful white teeth in all of Israel." No, it was predominately by their faith that Jesus identified people. We cannot avoid the fact that faith is intricately woven into the very fabric of Christianity. Abraham blazed a trail of faith that every Christian is called to follow.

In a sense, faith stands as the universal currency of the kingdom of heaven. What awesome news for those who fail to meet the cultural standards of our world! Are you less than stellar in appearance or popularity? You can be a person of faith! Did you grow up in a bad neighborhood on the wrong side of the railroad tracks? You can release His favor through faith! Do you lack athletic or artistic ability? You can receive God's empowering gifts through faith! Are you short of the intelligence or skills needed to succeed according to this world's standards? You can be a champion of faith!

If our faith is never stretched, it is likely an indication that we are failing to pursue God. During a profound moment, Jesus once told His followers not to work for physical food, but rather for eternal provision (see John 6:25-29). Whether confused or upset, I do not know, but they countered with a question of their own: "What shall we do, so that we may work the works of God?" Surprisingly, Jesus responded with, "This is the work of God, that you believe in Him whom He has sent."

Jesus was in a sense saying, "Don't be common laborers. Switch careers and be believers! Don't expend all of your energies to fill your stomachs. Feed your souls on Me, the Bread of Life! Don't walk by sight. Live by faith!"

The foundation and essence of life is an absolute trust in our Creator. Redemption and peace with God are impossible apart from faith. Further still, faith opens the door for intimacy with our heavenly Father; for without trust, intimacy is but a vaporous mist. Only through faith are we able to constantly abide in God's life-giving grace. And only genuine faith will produce real and lasting spiritual fruit. Faith matters.

Many of us struggle to understand the relationship between repentance and faith with regard to the gospel. Repentance, I have been told, is a "work" and therefore unnecessary for salvation. This confused me until I came to understand that the gospel isn't about repentance *and* faith but repentance *to* faith. When we repent as an integral part of the salvation process, we turn from all things that exalt self above God. This includes self-centeredness, self-determination, and self-sufficiency as part of a list too long to fully identify. In essence, to repent is to turn from pride to faith. True faith, it seems, is the only effective antidote for our stupid human pride; a life dependent on God must fully replace one of independent self-sufficiency.

This is part of what I believe Jesus was trying to communicate through John 6:25-29. Self-sufficiency demands that we provide for our own needs. In contrast, faith places the burden of provision squarely on God's more-than-capable shoulders. Does this mean that we should quit our jobs, or allow laziness to swallow our productivity? Not at all! We, however, must place everything in its proper perspective. Only through a faith-filled dependence on our faithful God are we able to break our constant preoccupation with the physical—and therefore temporary—aspects of life. These changes do not take place naturally or easily, which is why trusting God needs to become a career rather than a hobby.

PROBING QUESTIONS

Why do we tend to think that blessing and difficulty are mutually exclusive?

Why are trust and intimacy inseparable?

What is the primary area of your life in which you struggle to trust God?

ACTION STEP

Take some time today to deliberately encourage two other people in their faith.

CLOSING PRAYER

Heavenly Father, I want to launch out fully into my new career. Please open my eyes to Your true character and to the smear campaign against You. I ask that You write Your words upon my heart and make me to be a person of unshakeable faith.

FURTHER READING

Habakkuk 2:4; John 6:26-35; Romans 4:13-25

CHAPTER FIFTEEN
WHAT IS IT (THAT GOD SEEKS TO ACCOMPLISH)?

We want God to provide more so we need Him less.
–Mark Batterson, pastor and author

And when the dew had gone up, there was on the face of the wilderness a fine, flake-like thing, fine as frost on the ground. When the people of Israel saw it, they said to one another, "What is it?" For they did not know what it was. And Moses said to them, "It is the bread that the LORD has given you to eat. This is what the LORD has commanded: 'Gather of it, each one of you, as much as he can eat. You shall each take an omer, according to the number of the persons that each of you has in his tent.'" And the people of Israel did so. They gathered, some more, some less. But when they measured it with an omer, whoever gathered much had nothing left over, and whoever gathered little had no lack. Each of them gathered as much as he could eat. And Moses said to them, "Let no one leave any of it over till the morning." But they did not listen to Moses. Some left part of it till the morning, and it bred worms and stank. And Moses was angry with them.

EXODUS 16:14-20 (ESV)

"We need a plan!" I announced as my wife rolled her eyes. We each have our quirks and tendencies; over time those who know us well can accurately predict our reactions in any given situation. For me, planning is an important issue. I like to be prepared, mostly because I've encountered too many situations where a lack of preparation proved costly in one way or another. All plans, however, are not the same. We can plan with wisdom in an effort to meet anticipated needs—like saving money for a large purchase, instead of being forced to borrow. Or we can plan as we seek a sense of security—as in hoarding as much as possible in fear of what tomorrow may bring. The former type of planning can lead to a truly improved quality of life, while the latter will eventually turn foul and stink.

The word *manna* can be loosely translated as: *what is it?* God's people were simply trying to comprehend what He was doing. His provision of daily manna highlights an essential dimension of our heavenly Father's interaction with His children: He ever seeks to develop faith in the hearts of His people. We, on the other hand, seek security apart from Him, to the point of despising a lifestyle that requires any type of meaningful dependence upon our Creator. How many Christians pray, "Give us this day our daily bread," every Sunday in church, but give little thought to what they are asking? If any of us had penned that prayer, we would be asking for enough "daily" bread to last through the end of our lives. Let's not delude ourselves—very few of us honestly believe that we can rely on God day by day for our provision.

Understand that this is not a clarion call for all who profess Christ to cancel their insurance policies, or give up their retirement plans in mindless obedience to a misappropriated concept. Some of these things may actually be part of God's plan to provide for us. Like I previously mentioned, planning for prudence is not the same as planning for security. It is, however, essential that we align ourselves with God's kingdom paradigm in our day-to-day objectives. Otherwise we will find ourselves working against what our loving Father seeks to accomplish in our lives.

Honestly answer, if you will, this vital question: Where is my sense of security rooted? In my checking account balance? In my investments? In my family? In my friends? In my significant other? In my company? In my government? In myself? While none of these are bad within themselves, they become idolatrous—and offensive to God—when they replace Him as our primary source of security.

What in this world is truly secure? We now understand the frailty of the stock market like never before. We have learned in recent years that an outwardly healthy business or investment company may be a total sham. We've witnessed real estate collapses followed by a glut of foreclosures. And government securities, it seems, aren't nearly as secure as once thought. Money hidden in the mattress can quickly become worthless under the burden of runaway inflation. Our most secure investment is probably gold, but even gold is subject to price fluctuations and theft.

I sometimes lament that Debi and I failed to purchase and accumulate gold in the days when it was relatively inexpensive. The demands of rearing a family and the need to help care for my aging mother hindered us from squirreling away very many financial resources. Further still, we made the decision that I would walk away from a well-paying career as a chemist to live by faith as a campus minister. Yet when I begin to regret our failure to purchase gold, without fail, the Holy Spirit reminds me that in giving of ourselves to others, and learning to live by faith in the process, we have purchased golden treasures in heaven that can never be corrupted or stolen.

As humans, we naturally attempt to establish a sense of security from earthly things. Rather than being generous givers in the image of our Father, we err by holding tightly to that which has no value in the eyes of eternity. God's agenda, on the other hand, involves training us to trust Him with childlike dependence. In this case, ignorance of God's design is anything but bliss.

What Is It? I understand that manna is most often used as a metaphor to illustrate the importance of a daily time in the Bible as we feed on Christ as the Bread of Life—and I would never argue against such a use. But manna also paints a poignant picture of the importance of learning to trust God day by day. Let us not foolishly ignore this second, essential application.

PROBING QUESTIONS

Why do we so often seek to find security in earthly things?

How does seeking security in earthly things have the potential to damage a person's walk with God?

Where is the line between wisely saving and foolishly hoarding?

ACTION STEP

Take some time to evaluate your personal finances. Are you wisely saving? Are you foolishly hoarding? Make appropriate adjustments that you believe would honor God.

CLOSING PRAYER

Lord, open my eyes to see the insecurity of this world in light of the deep, deep confidence that can be found only in You.

FURTHER READING

Matthew 6:7-34; Luke 12:13-21; 1 Peter 1:3-12; Revelation 3:14-22

CHAPTER SIXTEEN
THE OBEDIENCE OF FAITH

The Bible recognizes no faith that does not lead to obedience, nor does it recognize any obedience that does not spring from faith. The two are at opposite sides of the same coin.
                                    –A.W. Tozer, pastor and author

---

By faith Abraham obeyed when he was called to go out to a place that he was to receive as an inheritance. And he went out, not knowing where he was going.
                                    HEBREWS 11:8 (ESV)

Is there any aspect of the gospel that causes more confusion than the relationship between faith, grace, love, and works? I don't think so. Ask thirty professing Christians how these things relate to one another, and you will probably get twenty-nine and a half different answers. But is seeking to clearly understand these concepts really worth the hassle? Let's just say that the difference can be life or death!

The Apostle Paul wrote in Colossians 1:6 that the gospel was "bearing fruit and increasing" wherever the grace of God was understood in truth. Grace, it appears, produces fruit—specifically the fruit of the Spirit (Galatians 5:22-23). If genuine fruit is not being borne, it is safe to say that the gospel of grace is not being properly understood or applied to daily life.

When we consider the sheer volume of teaching and the vast array of multimedia resources available to the Western church, it is difficult to believe that any of us would lack a clear understanding of such important concepts. But we do! We need only open our eyes to see the precipitous decline of the Christian church in the Western world as evidence. Does that mean that developing nations have a clearer understanding of the gospel? Not necessarily. It is simply an indication that those in the Western church are doing a poorer job of *living* by faith.

The essence of the relationship between faith, grace, love, and works is progressive. Upon hearing the word of God, we respond with faith. That faith introduces us to the empowering grace of our Lord and Savior. Through abiding in grace, the fruit of love begins to grow and develop in our hearts. And finally, love cannot help but express itself in works of obedience.

I understand that this perspective is over-simplified in that grace is multifaceted and must precede faith in some capacities. Otherwise, we would never take an interest in God, or have any faith to believe. Still, this simplified explanation has some merit. The bottom line is that even though we can never be saved by our good works, true faith will always produce love-motivated action. Good deeds are not a guaranteed indicator of faith, but an absence of good works serves as clear evidence that faith is lacking.

For almost two thousand years, Paul's letter to the Romans has stood as the definitive book of the Bible in presenting the gospel. I find it interesting that Romans begins and ends with Paul addressing the faith/obedience relationship:

> . . . *concerning His Son . . . through whom we have received grace and apostleship to bring about the obedience of faith among all the Gentiles for His name's sake.* Romans 1:3-5 (NASB)

> . . . *but now is manifested, and by the Scriptures of the prophets, according to the commandment of the eternal God, has been made known to all the nations, leading to obedience of faith.* Romans 16:26 (NASB)

Do you see it? Paul's "grace" letter to the Romans begins and ends with references to the "obedience of faith." Biblical faith should never be confused with some type of mental gymnastics where we cerebrally affirm a belief in God but never fully act upon those beliefs.

But what does all of this have to do with the wilderness? More than one might think. Abraham took a huge risk, leaving the familiar (stepping out of his *comfort zone*, if you will) and obeying God by venturing into unknown territory. What followed wasn't always pleasant. There were probably times when Abraham wondered if he had really been blessed by his Creator. How is it that blessings can sometimes feel like curses?

When we survey the horizon and all looks barren and bleak; when dark storm clouds begin to brew, when the thunder booms, the winds blow, and the flooding rains fall; do we genuinely believe that God is leading us for our good? Confidence in His faithful love can indeed mark the difference between life or death.

Abraham believed—and so he obeyed by venturing out into the wilderness. Amazing blessings followed in their appropriate time. Sadly, an entire generation of his descendants followed God into the wilderness, where all except Joshua and Caleb perished because they refused to believe.

Disobedience will do nothing to hasten the end of a wilderness journey. In fact, far too many of our problems stem from a failure to fully trust our heavenly Father through the difficulties and trials of life. It is not uncommon for us to fail to obey God because we are not fully surrendered to His will. And why do we fail to fully surrender to His will? Generally, it is because we don't believe in the depths of our hearts that, regardless of outward appearances, He never fails to keep our best interests in mind.

I am not suggesting that we act foolishly or shun all sense of responsibility, but rather that a wise approach to navigating the wilderness involves investigating root issues and not simply focusing on outward symptoms. Is it possible that our struggles reveal an area of disobedience in our lives—one that continually plagues us because we don't really know and trust God as much as we say we do?

PROBING QUESTIONS

How are faith, grace, love, and works related?

How does the absence of good works serve as evidence that faith is lacking?

Why is it important to examine these issues in our lives over a period of time rather than by taking a snapshot of any given moment?

ACTION STEP

Identify, and trace back to the roots, an area of your life in which you feel you may have been disobedient to God. Does the problem have anything to do with a failure to trust God? Consider how you can seek to deliberately trust your heavenly Father through similar circumstances that may arise in the future.

CLOSING PRAYER

Father, please teach me how to abide in Your grace so that I might be a living expression of Your love.

FURTHER READING

1 Corinthians 15:1-10; Colossians 1:3-6; James 2:14-26

CHAPTER SEVENTEEN
AM I DOING SOMETHING WRONG?

Doubt discovers difficulties which it never solves; it creates hesitancy, despondency, despair. Its progress is the decay of comfort, the death of peace. "Believe!" is the word which speaks life into a man, but doubt nails down his coffin.

—Charles Spurgeon, pastor and author

Abiathar told David that Saul had killed the priests of the LORD. Then David said to Abiathar, "I knew that Doeg the Edomite was there that day and that he was sure to report to Saul. I myself am responsible for the lives of everyone in your father's family. Stay with me. Don't be afraid, for the one who wants to take my life wants to take your life. You will be safe with me."

1 SAMUEL 22:21-23 (HCSB)

Wilderness seasons are often times of double-mindedness; we tend to question almost everything we "thought" we heard God speak on the mountaintop. We wonder if we are really up for the tasks before us. Or perhaps, we are sinful and broken beyond the measure of most other Christians—those have-it-all-together people we know only from a distance. We can't help but think that if we were doing things right, we would not be in the wilderness. Ironically, it is such double-minded questioning that unnecessarily extends our unwanted wilderness experiences.

Thankfully, these types of struggles put us in good company. David was anointed by the prophet Samuel as the future king of

Israel, and yet, virtually all of his circumstances appeared to speak otherwise. David, however, understood the nature of his covenantal relationship with God. Rather than sinking into the self-defeating world of double-mindedness, he learned to deal humbly and honestly with his struggles, and then to move on.

I am no stranger to double-mindedness. When Debi and I first began our relationship, we thought that something might be wrong with us as a couple. As we interacted with other Christian couples our age, we noticed that they argued—a lot. For reasons I still don't completely understand, we got along very well; arguments between us were quite rare. Before long, we began to second-guess our relationship. Perhaps we weren't being real, or genuine, or honest. Was it possible that we were somehow denying our true thoughts and feelings? Thankfully, over time we came to realize that our relationship was indeed healthy.

I had similar self-doubts during my years as a campus minister—only they were much more numerous and over a far longer period of time. We tried our best to honor God and walk with integrity in how we did ministry. That was all well and good—except for the fact that the size of our fellowship never grew the way I thought that it should. Wherever I turned, it seemed that I encountered other campus ministries much larger and much more dynamic than ours. The result was that I could not stop second-guessing our ministry efforts.

Through our more than sixteen years of campus ministry, I had serious doubts about both my personal abilities and our ministry plan. If we were doing it right, I reasoned, our attendance would be much larger. And yet, our main group meeting never averaged more than about forty-five students. (If we consider the entire length of time we did college ministry, we were actually privileged to influence many more people than I once realized.)

There were things I could have done to draw a larger crowd—like attempting to make the unpleasant aspects of the gospel more palatable, or making our ministry more people-centered instead of Christ-centered. (I am by no means suggesting that all large ministries are compromising the gospel!) The first meetings of the fall semester were always the most important for growing a campus fellowship, but without fail, my first message of the school-year tended to be more challenging than welcoming (not that it was unwelcoming). Those messages had a negative impact on the size of our group as many new visitors failed to return, although many did come back and get involved during their junior and senior years. I could not help but share what I felt God was speaking—and what the students genuinely needed to hear.

About four years after we left college ministry to devote ourselves to the work of Search for Me Ministries, we held a reunion with a group of our former students. During our time together, I found myself deeply touched as person after person shared how his or her life had been radically impacted by our ministry. After graduating and moving on with life, they discovered that very few of their new friends had received the same depth of foundation that they had received under our care. That weekend served as a powerful reminder that we were doing a lot more right than I ever allowed myself to believe.

The Christian life always operates by faith. Even when we fall short, we must approach our error or inability with faith, believing that God is greater than our shortcomings. If we truly know our identity in the eyes of our heavenly Father, we will feel no need to measure up to worldly standards of success. If we submit honestly to His lordship, we will tune our hearts and ears to His still, small voice. And if we genuinely understand His grace, we will embrace His corrective guidance as loving discipline, rather than as a condemning assault.

After wrestling with double-mindedness for much of my life, I have come to conclude that it accomplishes nothing of value. If anything, constant second-guessing is highly detrimental. Of course, we need personal honesty and humble, teachable spirits. If, however, we are to move forward in this journey with God, self-doubt, double-mindedness, and condemnation we can—and must—do without.

PROBING QUESTIONS

Is there an area of self-doubt or double-mindedness that has plagued you for any length of time?

Can you identify its origins?

How can double-mindedness serve to extend an unwanted wilderness experience?

ACTION STEP

Identify an area of life in which you are double-minded and begin to apply promises from God's word to that area of doubt. (Appendix I will provide you with a good starting point.)

CLOSING PRAYER

Lord God, I desire to honor You in all that I do. Please grant me the grace to effectively put double-mindedness in the rearview mirror of my life.

FURTHER READING

Hebrews 11:1-6; James 1:1-8; 1 John 5:14-15

CHAPTER EIGHTEEN
FRAGILE SHIELDS OF WISHFUL THINKING

Daily living by faith on Christ is what makes the difference between the sickly and the healthy Christian, between the defeated and the victorious saint.

–A.W. Pink, pastor and author

**Joseph is a fruitful bough,
a fruitful bough by a spring;
his branches run over the wall.
The archers bitterly attacked him,
shot at him, and harassed him severely,
yet his bow remained unmoved;
his arms were made agile
by the hands of the Mighty One of Jacob.**

GENESIS 49:22-24 (ESV)

When we were kids, my cousin Michael and I used to love mid-winter Saturday afternoon television flicks. Some were westerns, some monster movies, some science fiction. All involved action, pitting the forces of good against evil in a fight to the death. We learned that in the days of old, long before guns arrived on the scene, the bow and arrow was often the weapon of choice. An excellent archer, such as Robin Hood, could silently take down an enemy in the twitch of a cat's whisker.

The bow and arrow was used during biblical times, but the Scriptures also speak of arrows in a figurative sense. Jacob, for example, told how Joseph was severely harassed by archers even though we have no record of this literally happening. Regardless of our personal perspectives on spiritual warfare, there is an evil archer (we call him "Satan") and one of his favorite weapons is a flaming arrow intended to strike at the very heart of the Christian life (see Ephesians 6:10-17). When the forces of evil ambush us—often from the shadows—our primary source of protection is our own personal "shield of faith" which God gives us the wisdom and strength to utilize.

I keep returning to this issue of faith because, as a general rule, the Western church tends to live more in the realm of wishful thinking than genuine faith. We have had it fairly easy for a long time and are not doing all that well in dealing with the hardships now coming upon us. How we perceive God at work—or not at work—in the midst of our circumstances can make all of the difference. Those who seek to participate in the advance of God's coming kingdom cannot do so without living by faith.

There was one particular time during my senior year of college when I found myself struggling with a wave of anxiety regarding my future. I remember feeling as though I had a choice in how I handled the weight of my concerns, but my natural tendency was to fear, and so fear I did. One evening, as I worried my way along a cold, dark street, one of Satan's flaming arrows flew out of the shadows and hit me squarely in the chest, initiating an especially unpleasant illness that lasted for several days. Even though flaming arrows and shields of faith are invisible to the naked eye, that experience—and many others since—taught me that even though something may be described figuratively in the Bible, it need not be imaginary. Spiritual warfare is an unfortunate reality.

Christians in the Western world are under siege, and it is not just by atheists or political rivals. The real problem lies in the seeds of unbelief that we have allowed to sprout and take root in our hearts. When our enemies fire at us with their flaming arrows—as enemies are known to do—we find ourselves susceptible, too often trying to block violent spiritual attacks with nothing more than *Fragile Shields of Wishful Thinking*.

Why is it that we are so easily angered? Why do we allow fear, cynicism, and bitterness to take root in our hearts? Why, when in the midst of a wilderness experience, do we constantly fall prey to discouragement? We lose heart and become depressed as a result of our reaction to circumstances that are not what we want (or think they should be). We hold onto an idealized form of reality, while growing increasingly negative in our view of life. The cumulative effect can be a wilderness of our own creation.

All of this means that we each need to periodically reevaluate our approach to life to ensure that we process *everything* through the eye of faith. No matter what our age, or the extent of our Christian experience, we cannot flourish by merely having, or possessing, faith; we must *live* by faith. Christianity is a full-time faith-walk— not a comfort-walk, not a security-walk, not a spectator-walk, but a faith-walk. Until we come to grips with this reality—that every facet of life must be processed through the eye of faith—we not only will be discouraged by feeling abandoned in the wilderness; we also will remain susceptible to Satan's weapon of choice.

It is sometimes necessary to slow the pace of life to prayerfully reflect on issues that may be bothering us. Concern for a loved one, a seemingly unanswered prayer, frustration with our government, or the fear of moving in a new direction in life can all be things that weigh on us over the course of time. We begin to feel burdened without really knowing why. But as we take the time to pray and reflect, we can better identify specific issues, surrender them to God, and deliberately exercise faith. The burdens will begin to lift and we will find the strength that we need to raise our protective shields.

Our enemies will never hesitate to exploit any weakness on our part. If we hope to extinguish evil arrows burning with the fires of fear, worry, and doubt, then we need to have our shields of faith in fighting shape—and in use.

PROBING QUESTIONS

Can you recall a time when you were hit with a flaming arrow from the evil one because your shield of faith was down?

What is the difference between a genuine shield of faith and a *Fragile Shield of Wishful Thinking*?

Why is *living* by faith rarely on our agendas?

ACTION STEP
Spend some time alone with God reflecting and praying about three things that may be burdening you. Displace the weight of each concern with a Scripture that strengthens your faith in that particular area of life.

CLOSING PRAYER
Lord, help me to know that faith is much more than a mental exercise. Search my heart and cleanse any unbelief so that my shield of faith is impenetrable.

FURTHER READING
Psalms 139:23-24; Romans 1:16-17; Ephesians 6:10-17

CHAPTER NINETEEN
SWEETENING BITTER WATERS

Acrid bitterness inevitably seeps into the lives of people who harbor grudges and suppress anger, and bitterness is always a poison. It keeps your pain alive instead of letting you deal with it and get beyond it. Bitterness sentences you to relive the hurt over and over.

–Lee Strobel, journalist and author

Then Moses led Israel from the Red Sea, and they went out into the wilderness of Shur; and they went three days in the wilderness and found no water. When they came to Marah, they could not drink the waters of Marah, for they were bitter; therefore it was named Marah. So the people grumbled at Moses, saying, "What shall we drink?" Then he cried out to the LORD, and the LORD showed him a tree; and he threw it into the waters, and the waters became sweet.
EXODUS 15:22-25 (NASB)

Seeking to communicate the power of a thankful heart to a group of college students, I once passed out cookies that had been baked without sweetener. Feeling a little too much pleasure, I watched their feigned attempts at courtesy, betrayed by the sour looks of such an unpleasant taste. Life without a thankful heart is a bitter pill indeed.

In less favorable circumstances, I once used Exodus 15:22-25 during a memorial service for a college student who had tragically overdosed on drugs. Parents send their children off to college to take a step forward in life, not to die. It is difficult to find appropriate words in such circumstances. In that particular situation, I explained that the tree God showed Moses served as a metaphor for the cross. Through the sacrificial death and resurrection of Christ, God is able to sweeten the bitter waters of our lives.

I would like to say that only those who disobey God will experience bitter waters. I cannot say that. Simply by nature of the fact that we live in a fallen world, we will encounter bitter waters even if we live in total obedience to God's will. Ever since the day in the garden of Eden when death entered the human scene, love and pain have been mysteriously bound. As much as we would like to believe differently, nothing we can do or believe will remove death from this side of heaven. The bitter waters of life, however, need not remain undrinkable.

My own flow of bitter waters has been anything but minimal, yet as I look back over the course of my life, they no longer taste unpalatable. It's not that the memories are gone—I could relive just about every painful episode if I so chose—but that God has done such an amazing work in the emotions of my heart. I no longer see my past as a wilderness wasteland, full of injustice, and lacking in meaning or purpose.

Thankfully, experiencing God's healing touch is not unique to me. Throughout my life, I have met many other Christians who have also experienced deep pain but emerged as champions over bitterness. Perhaps no story strikes me as much as Joye's—a young pregnant woman who was raped at knifepoint by an intruder while her husband was at work. A mere three years later, I heard Joye explain that God had brought such a measure of healing that she felt as though she were speaking of someone else when telling her own story.

What made the difference? How could Joye's horror turn so fully into inspiration? In a generic sense, we can say that it was God, which would undoubtedly be true. Still, in the midst of her emotional nightmare Joye made calculated decisions that enabled her to abide in the healing power of the cross. She began by choosing not to confine herself to a wilderness of isolation. In spite of this man's self-absorbed actions, Joye chose not to follow suit. Instead, she recognized that there were others who truly cared about her. Isolating herself from human conduits of God's love would have been a grave mistake, she felt. I am sure that many tears were shed as Joye initially shared her painful experience with a few trusted friends, but their unconditional love soothed her distressed soul.

Joye and her husband, John, also made a deliberate decision to forgive the assailant. Yes, they went through a wide range of expected emotions such as sadness and anger; and, yes, it took time to allow such feelings to run their course. But in the end, they chose to let go of their bitterness, resting in full confidence that our heavenly Father is more than able to redeem the fruit of humanity's self-absorption. In a very real sense, in spite of her struggles, every step Joye made was the result of a decision to focus on and trust in God's goodness, fully yielding to His healing touch. In Joye's case, bitterness paid a visit to the threshold of her heart, but she refused to open the door and make it a welcome friend.

I cannot help but contrast Joye's experience with that of another Christian woman I once met. Having been deeply hurt at a young age, twenty years removed she tearfully spoke of her pain as though it had pierced her heart only the day prior. In a sense, her bitter pain had become a faithful companion, never straying far through the course of her entire life.

Forgiveness and thankfulness—at first glance these two traveling companions appear to be unrelated. But when all is said and done, both serve as invaluable expressions of faith in our ever faithful God. Are the waters of your life bitter? Choose to forgive. Choose to express thankfulness in God's goodness. Life's circumstances will never be able to dam the sweet flow of His healing grace.

PROBING QUESTIONS

How are forgiveness and thankfulness related?

More than anything else, what tends to make you bitter?

What are some practical steps we can take to help us access God's healing grace in the midst of deep emotional hurt?

ACTION STEP
Make a list of any people that you need to forgive. Turn your heart toward God in prayer and verbally forgive each one by name. Thank God for the grace to forgive, and that He will use all that was meant for evil for good.

CLOSING PRAYER
Heavenly Father, I thank You that You sent Your Son to die on that terrible cross that I might be forgiven of my sins. Help me to always extend that same grace by forgiving those who hurt me and my loved ones.

FURTHER READING
Matthew 18:21-35; Philippians 4:4-7; 1 Thessalonians 5:12-22

CHAPTER TWENTY
BACK TO EGYPT? NEVER!

Our yesterdays present irreparable things to us; it is true that we have lost opportunities which will never return, but God can transform this destructive anxiety into a constructive thoughtfulness for the future. Let the past sleep, but let it sleep on the bosom of Christ. Leave the Irreparable Past in His hands, and step out into the Irresistible Future with Him.
> –Oswald Chambers, evangelist and Christian educator

Then the whole community broke into loud cries, and the people wept that night. All the Israelites complained about Moses and Aaron, and the whole community told them, "If only we had died in the land of Egypt, or if only we had died in this wilderness! Why is the LORD bringing us into this land to die by the sword? Our wives and little children will become plunder. Wouldn't it be better for us to go back to Egypt?" So they said to one another, "Let's appoint a leader and go back to Egypt."

NUMBERS 14:1-4 (HCSB)

Will any of us ever have an unwanted wilderness experience in which we, like the Israelites, are not tempted to give up and turn back? My early years before becoming a Christian were particularly painful. Then, as I contemplated embracing Jesus as my Lord and Savior, I somehow knew that such a radical decision was going to cost me in lost friendships. Close friendships. Friendships that mattered a great deal. Friendships that had provided a sense of support and security through some particularly vulnerable years. Just the thought of losing valued friendships made moving forward in Christ all the more difficult.

Looking back on that painful separation, I can see now that I needed to let go of the old in order to fully embrace the new. God had a calling and destiny for me that was very different from anything I or my friends had ever known. I needed the time and freedom to become fully established in my new faith. And while I would never say that every new believer needs to cut off all old relationships, there are times when this is the best course of action—especially if those old relationships are somehow hindering or, worse yet, corrupting our newfound walk with God.

When we walk through a door into another room, we must, by necessity, leave the previous room. If the lighting is different, with the first room being very dark, for example, our view of the new room is influenced by the dilation of our pupils. What had helped us to see more effectively in one room momentarily blinds us in the next. If only making emotional transitions were so simple—and so short-lived! Why is it that we have such a difficult time letting go of the past?

Behavioral experts tell us that the early childhood years have a profound, lasting impact on our entire lives. Isn't it amazing how such a short period of time can impact decades of living? I think that the average Christian's view of life is sometimes defined more by his or her perspective of the past than by a clear understanding of God. In many ways, yesterday is all we know, with its subconscious messages continually sounding in our ears.

The future is unknown, the past familiar. When we do not know and understand the nature of God and how He operates, we will be tempted to choose a lost, but familiar yesterday over what we perceive as an unknown—and possibly scary—tomorrow. We can easily gauge the pain of the past—we've already experienced it. But the potential pain of the future? Well, if the past has been bad, the future just might be worse!

How do we make sense of this struggle? Why do we so strongly hold on to what was when we so desire a better tomorrow? The answer lies in how we process the difficulties of the wilderness. All too often, we are told, "Just get on with it! The past is history. It's time to forget what lies behind and move forward." But there is a problem and it's not a small one! The past isn't just history if it still negatively influences our current relationships. We can only move on to the future after we have learned to somehow reprocess the past through the light of God's love and faithfulness.

The Israelites in the wilderness could have looked at their current needs, remembered the pain and bondage of Egypt, and then focused on their faithful God to powerfully deliver and supernaturally provide for His children. By reframing their experiences, they would have been better able to put the pain of the past to rest—permanently.

Let's not be ignorant of God's wise and loving ways. He may sometimes use our wilderness experiences to bring painful memories to the surface, not to torment us, but to free us from their unhealthy influence. We need not dig up all of the old stuff buried in our emotional closets, but as we enter new spiritual territory, memories—both good and bad—will rise to the surface. Our task at hand, then, is to learn how to process our yesterdays through the lens of God's always faithful love.

God concerns Himself with more than your present and your future—He wants to redeem your memories as well. Surrender what once was into the loving hands of your heavenly Father, giving Him complete freedom to rewrite your perspective. Don't allow yourself to remain stuck in the mire from which you came. The bondage of your past offers no hope for your future.

PROBING QUESTIONS

Why are painful memories so often influential in shaping our view of the future?

What is the difference between simply forgetting the past and reframing our experiences?

What are some of the things we can do to help reframe the past?

ACTION STEP

Think of a painful memory and ask God to help you to reframe the experience through the eye of faith. Be sure to keep His love and faithfulness in the forefront of your mind.

CLOSING PRAYER

Lord Jesus, my heart longs to follow after You. Help me to let go of any pain from my past so that I can fully lay hold of the good things that You have planned for me.

FURTHER READING

Isaiah 42:1-9; John 6:60-69; Philippians 3:1-14

CHAPTER TWENTY-ONE
THE SECRET OF THE PSALMS

There are always uncertainties ahead, but there is always one certainty—God's will is good.

—Vernon Paterson, businessman

For the enemy has persecuted my soul;
He has crushed my life to the ground;
He has made me dwell in dark places, like those who have
long been dead.
Therefore my spirit is overwhelmed within me;
My heart is appalled within me.
I remember the days of old;
I meditate on all Your doings;
I muse on the work of Your hands.
I stretch out my hands to You;
My soul longs for You, as a parched land.
PSALMS 143:3-6 (NASB)

The Psalms—many of which were penned in the midst of a wilderness season—are full of all sorts of raw emotion that the authors seemed to have no fear of expressing. In the end, however, the picture of their intense struggles was always viewed through the greater backdrop of God's never-ending goodness. Many a Psalm begins with pain and agony but ends with rejoicing. The darkness isn't so dark when our thoughts are fixed on God's goodness.

Like anyone else, I have a story or two about navigating in the dark. On one particular occasion, I wanted to canoe the Conemaugh

River—a rather popular float for those from the Pittsburgh area. I did a little research before the trek but not nearly enough. You can probably guess that some challenges resulted. Thankfully, Debi is a good sport—most of the time!

The plan was simple: after an outfitter dropped us off below the dam, I'd fish and Debi would read a cheesy Amish novel as we drifted the canoe a couple of miles down-river to our car. The weather was nice and a few other canoes somehow added to the serene feel of the experience. Unfortunately, the shadows were lengthening and I had severely underestimated the distance we needed to travel. Two or three miles from start to finish? Try six or seven!

The scenery around the river was both beautiful and peaceful, but as the day drew to a close, I felt the need to get moving down the river. I put away my rod and Debi her book, casually noting that we were now alone on the water. Grabbing the paddles we leisurely worked our way downstream, taking time to soak in the beauty of nature. The river was indeed a gem.

As time passed, a sense of foreboding began to grow in my heart. With the murky darkness enveloping our surroundings, we soon forgot about the setting and began to paddle more intensely toward our destination. Suddenly, the journey ceased to be fun. We could barely see, and our no-longer-youthful arms tired quickly. Every bend in the river promised hope, but somehow left us wondering what we had gotten ourselves into. (Actually, it was more like: "Robert, what have *you* gotten us into? Next time I'll stay at home and you can bring one of your friends!") Utilizing my outstanding grasp of the obvious, I realized that spending several more hours lost on a river in total darkness would not be good for my marriage. Fearful thoughts tried to overrun my mind, and I began to doubt whether we could even recognize the boat launch through the thick darkness.

Thankfully, in the end, we did recognize the launch and were able to pull the boat out of the water without a problem. I even felt as though it had been a fun adventure, although I am not exactly sure that my semi-patient wife agreed. Perhaps, that is because she still refuses to take another canoe float with her husband!

There are times in our spiritual lives when we feel as though we are traveling in the dark, as if the promises of God don't apply to us—or even worse—appear to be totally senseless. It is during these confusing circumstances that we must focus on the character of God, specifically His goodness. God's goodness is like the North Star—a faithfully fixed point of light in dark, unknown territory.

Many years ago I found myself sitting in a hospital waiting room with a friend whose wife had suddenly and mysteriously gone into convulsions. Doctors did not know what was happening and were not optimistic about her survival. Jack, the father of four children (one newly born), was at a loss on how to handle the situation. As several of us sat quietly, doing our awkward best to be supportive, he turned to me and asked if I could make any sense of the situation. I couldn't, I replied, but of one thing I was certain: God is good and worthy of the full weight of our trust—regardless of how hopeless or confusing our circumstances might appear. Miraculously, Cathy survived the ordeal with no long-term effects.

Since that night, I have turned toward this foundational truth for light and hope during dark times: regardless of what I can see or understand, God is absolutely faithful and always worthy of my complete confidence. Yes, I prefer to understand my current circumstances (of which this book provides ample evidence), but I do not need to understand *everything* in order to trust my good and faithful Father.

Further still, verbally proclaiming God's goodness as an expression of our faith in the midst of dark times is a powerful way to both honor God and to lift our spirits. Praise, worship, and confession of His word can have an almost magical effect on the human heart. What was once dark becomes light, despair can't help but yield to hopefulness, and barren dryness soon gives birth to a spring of life.

Do you feel as though you are navigating dark and confusing territory? Rivet your focus on God's stellar character! No, go a step further; sing or simply declare out loud His goodness. You will soon see an amazingly bright light of hope, even in dark places.

PROBING QUESTIONS

How does focusing on God's goodness help us to navigate confusing times?

Why is it so important for God's character to be the foundation of our trust in His promises?

How does expressing God's goodness force darkness to yield to light?

ACTION STEP

Spend some time this week reading several of the Psalms out loud.

CLOSING PRAYER

Lord, I thank You that I can trust You even when I don't understand my circumstances. Help me to know Your goodness as the foundation of my life.

FURTHER READING

Psalms 56, 57, 63; Philippians 4:8-9

CHAPTER TWENTY-TWO
THE GOD FACTOR

Faith is a reasoning trust, a trust which reckons thoughtfully and confidently upon the trustworthiness of God.
—John Stott, Christian scholar and author

Saul went on one side of the mountain, and David and his men on the other side of the mountain. And David was hurrying to get away from Saul. As Saul and his men were closing in on David and his men to capture them, a messenger came to Saul, saying, "Hurry and come, for the Philistines have made a raid against the land." So Saul returned from pursuing after David and went against the Philistines. Therefore that place was called the Rock of Escape.

1 SAMUEL 23:26-28 (ESV)

Mark and Sara were mired in the midst of difficult financial circumstances—most of us can relate. Having recently moved from one state to another due to an employment change, their financial landscape looked bleak for the next several months. Repeatedly, they crunched the numbers, hoping that perhaps they had made a mistake. Their efforts were to no avail—they had too many bills and not enough income. The only logical option was to somehow borrow enough money to make it through to their next paycheck.

Sara approached Debi and me to ask our opinion about their best course of action. Should they try to borrow money from her parents, put the expenses on a credit card, or borrow from their

401(k) plan? Each option had obvious drawbacks, but they needed to do something to navigate their grim financial landscape.

"Have you considered asking God for help?" I queried. Sara stood there staring at us with a far off look—the kind of facial expression a person gets when confronted with a new and different idea. A slight smile formed as a fresh gleam of hope entered her heart. No, they hadn't really considered prayer for provision as a reasonable approach, and the thought of their heavenly Father providing for their needs was certainly more favorable than borrowing money. Mark and Sara had been momentarily blinded to what I like to call *The God Factor*.

Several weeks later we spoke with Sara; her face beamed with excitement as she explained how God had mysteriously provided for their every need. The numbers didn't make sense on paper, but they actually had an excess in their checking account at the end of the month. Just as God had delivered David when fleeing from Saul in the wilderness; just as He has miraculously intervened for so many of His children through the course of history; so the heavenly Father had delivered Mark and Sara from their financial jam.

As humans, we have a natural tendency to lean heavily, if not exclusively, on our own abilities to figure things out. This tendency is especially pronounced with highly intelligent people (as I learned firsthand through my years as a campus minister). For a long time now, I've considered myself to be a low-grade intellectual— somewhat of the same magnitude as a low-grade fever. What a challenge it has been to work with people whose mental capacities are often far beyond my own! Regardless, however, of their intellectual prowess, the same scenario presented itself time and time again. A student would invariably be trapped in some type of undesirable circumstance, for which no amount of brainstorming could produce a favorable solution. Discouragement and despair then followed— often to the point of hopelessness.

Some of their problems were self-inflicted due to self-centered behavior, or a lack of godly wisdom (wisdom and intelligence are very different from one another). Other unfavorable circumstances were the consequences, not of their own sins, but of the actions of others over whom they had no control. Of course, there are always those painful situations that are simply the fruit of living in a fallen world. Life is rarely one-dimensional, and so combinations of factors are often to blame. I knew of at least two or three intellectually brilliant students who were so blind to God's hope that they considered suicide to be their only "logical" (the taking of one's own life is anything but logical) option.

At this point, some readers may think that I am leading them to the entrance of a well-worn path marked by a sign reading, "Don't ask questions! Just believe!" You know, that mindset where intelligent people are encouraged to stow their brains on a dusty shelf in order to blindly pursue God, to succumb to an existence where rational thought is to be treated like a deadly plague.

I have already mentioned that I consider myself to be a low-brow intellectual, so as a general rule, cranial activity is not something I discourage. Our problem is not rational thought but *self-trust*. Regardless of IQ, most people base their confidence on their own ability to see and understand. No matter what expression it takes, self-trust is a form of pride—a vice which is entirely offensive to our Creator. As long as our confidence is in our own selves, we will remain blind to the illumination of God's ways and susceptible to the dead end trails of human wisdom.

Asking questions is rarely a problem, but questioning with hearts full of doubt will create a wilderness desert of our own making. Faith in our loving Lord always serves as the foundation for true wisdom. Let us take care to distinguish between natural human thought and the wisdom of God.

If a wilderness season is to become a journey of transformation rather than a time lost in oblivion, something must change within us along the way, especially in the arena of self-trust as opposed to biblical faith. Our journeys must sometimes, then, by necessity, take us to places that don't make logical sense. Only in those dark valleys can we learn to account for *The God Factor*. Only then does the human heart begin to grasp that God is so much bigger than our circumstances, so much bigger than our ability to understand, and so much bigger than our pitiful solutions to complex issues.

Let us obediently move forward, step by step, even when our circumstances don't appear to make sense. If we are careful to account for the unseen *God Factor*, everything will come into focus in due season. He is, and always will be, our "Rock of Escape" from seemingly hopeless situations.

PROBING QUESTIONS
Can you recall a time in the past when you put your trust in your own wisdom instead of God's way of doing things? What was the outcome?

Why are we so prone toward self-trust?

Are you facing a current situation in which you have failed to fully account for *The God Factor*?

ACTION STEP
Identify an area of your life in which you may currently be operating by your own wisdom. Take some time to pray and ask God for His wisdom for the situation.

CLOSING PRAYER
Heavenly Father, I thank You that You alone are worthy to be the focus of my trust. Please forgive any misplaced trust in my heart and teach me to always look to You first in good times and in bad.

FURTHER READING
Proverbs 18:10-11, 28:26; Isaiah 55:6-13; Matthew 11:25-30

CHAPTER TWENTY-THREE
IS GOD CRUEL?

Just because it doesn't make sense to you doesn't mean it doesn't make sense.

–Adrian Rogers, pastor and author

The sons of Israel said to them, "Would that we had died by the LORD'S hand in the land of Egypt, when we sat by the pots of meat, when we ate bread to the full; for you have brought us out into this wilderness to kill this whole assembly with hunger."

EXODUS 16:3 (NASB)

Whether our musings are the size of a watermelon or a pea, too many of us have imbedded in our minds the idea that God has a cruel streak. The long and short of it is that we have a problem with ignorance. In a collective sense, we don't know God, we don't understand His ways, and we don't fully comprehend the nature of our sin-soaked world. The only way for our doubts to be erased is for each of us to become a theologian. The way that we view life, all that we do (and don't do), even our motivational desires, all find their roots in theology.

Many of us think, of course, that theology is the meat of scholars alone. All of that high, intelligent stuff is best left for those who have impressive titles and long lists of letters surrounding their names, who can explain the nuances of Greek grammar, and who use big, confusing words like *soteriology*. Or, so we think. We fail to recognize that *theology* is nothing more than *the study of God's nature and how He interacts with our world.*

While a few people deliberately take the time to search for truth, others simply swallow what they are told by the "experts" (an expert can be anybody whose opinion is trusted). Regardless of where we get our knowledge, every one of us is a theologian because every one of us has formed opinions about the nature of God and His interaction with people. The Israelites who came out of Egypt were theologians—they had opinions about how God interacts with humans—but their theology was dead wrong, and sent an entire generation to a wilderness graveyard. Can we see that every one of us needs to have an accurate perspective of God? Bad behavior is the result of bad theology.

It is a huge mistake to think that all theology must be complex. Our Creator is the God of the common laborer as well as the God of the scholar. For the most part, our explanation of spiritual things should be able to find accurate expression in common language. One simple way to guard against bad theology is to watch for what we might call "a spirit of elitism". An organization steeped in human wisdom will always be led by the elite—those untouchable, unreachable individuals who alone possess an intimate knowledge of God. This is not to say that Christian ministries and organizations are meant to be leaderless, or that leaders must be uneducated or ineffective to be humble, but that Christian leaders should always be servants who seek not to proclaim their own greatness, but to lift others to new heights.

Of one thing we can be sure: a seminary degree is not a prerequisite for procuring an accurate image of our Creator. Christian education is by no means problematic by nature; still, knowing and understanding God's ways is a matter of the heart as much as it is the mind. Thus, true knowledge of God comes as much by way of personal revelation from the Holy Spirit as it does through being taught by other people. I believe that, in addition to individual Bible reading and study, the most powerful learning environments are those in which teachable people receive accurate, life-giving instruction from humble teachers, processing what they learn in small, interactive groups.

Is there a more important arena of understanding than our perception of God? Who we believe God is—or isn't—influences everything we do. How many people run from God when they are struggling? How many have walked away from the Christian faith because the God of the Old Testament appears to be unjust? Many more profess a love for God—people who genuinely want to believe— but struggle with secret doubts because particular doctrines simply don't add up in their minds.

Knowing the character and nature of God is a prerequisite for knowing how God relates to humanity. Why? Because God's wisdom is far above human wisdom, His actions don't always make sense to us. If, however, we have an accurate perception of who God is, we can still live by faith—even when our circumstances don't seem to line up with our understanding.

I think that one of the greatest faith statements of the Bible was made by Job in the midst of unimaginably painful and confusing circumstances:

Though He slay me, I will hope in Him. Job 13:15a (NASB)

Job thought his situation was unfair. He could not see how the God he served would allow such horrible circumstances in the life of His faithful servant. And yet, Job knew the character of God, enabling him to stay the course through seemingly endless days of pain and confusion. In spite of his situation, Job knew that God was good and completely worthy of his trust. A generation of Israelites disbelieved and died in the wilderness because of their wrong theology; Job continued to believe in the midst of worse circumstances. Long before the pages of the Bible were penned, Job understood the character of God.

On an almost routine basis, I find myself saying, "God, I don't get it. I don't understand how this situation will work out, or what You want to accomplish in my life." In such situations, we must lay aside our preconceived notions to seek a clearer understanding of His character. He is who He is regardless of what we think, but it is always wise to avoid the temptation to try to remake God according to our own imaginations.

The wilderness, my friends, rarely makes sense. That is why we must all become theologians. The burden falls on us to dig deep into the Scriptures and to spend time praying at His feet, crying out to know Him and His ways. If, with honest and open hearts, we fervently seek to know God, He will be sure to reveal Himself to us, thereby establishing our faith on rock-solid ground.

PROBING QUESTIONS
Do you have a favorable or unfavorable view of the word *theology*? Why?

In what ways does our perspective of God's character impact practically every area of life?

Why is the state of a person's heart every bit as important as the mind when it comes to knowing God and understanding His ways?

ACTION STEP
Find and read an excellent book—such as *Knowledge of the Holy* by A.W. Tozer—that focuses on the character and nature of God. As you read the book, study the Scripture verses utilized by the author, praying for God to open your eyes to His true character.

CLOSING PRAYER
Heavenly Father, open my eyes that I might know You and see You for who You are.

FURTHER READING
Proverbs 25:2, Matthew 13:10-17; Luke 24:13-31; Ephesians 4:17-24

CHAPTER TWENTY-FOUR
BENCHMARKS IN THE WILDERNESS

Gather the riches of God's promises. Nobody can take away from you those texts from the Bible which you have learned by heart.
–Corrie Ten Boom, Holocaust survivor and inspirational speaker

---

"Have I not commanded you? Be strong and courageous! Do not tremble or be dismayed, for the LORD your God is with you wherever you go."
JOSHUA 1:9 (NASB)

Friends of ours once rented a house in rural western Pennsylvania. Nearby, sat a rather large stone with a *benchmark* disk permanently attached to the surface. Long before the GPS came into existence, the U.S. government embedded metal benchmarks as fixed points of reference to identify specific locations. Surveyors utilized them as guides to define property boundaries, while a confused traveler could use a benchmark to help establish a clear sense of direction.

A person wandering through a wilderness does not need to recognize *all* of the surrounding territory as long as he or she can identify at least one fixed point of reference. The ability to identify something—a mountain, for example—can not only provide confidence, but will eventually lead the way to civilization.

In a spiritual sense, we can find our way through confusing circumstances if we are able to locate reliable spiritual benchmarks—those fixed points of reference that remain rock-solid regardless of what is happening around us. We must note, however, that our ability to navigate the sometimes rugged terrain of life is only as effective as the standards by which we are guided. A benchmark must be set in stone if it is to weather the test of time. I once read of a mountain climber who anchored a disk in ice at the top of Mount McKinley. Not surprisingly, future climbers were unable to find the mark he had set. Ice may be hard, but it is highly uncertain. Perhaps you, too, have seen news reports of an unsuspecting driver crashing into a storefront, running into a field, or even drowning in a lake while following the directions of an inaccurate GPS unit. A worthy benchmark must provide a reliable standard by which our situation can be accurately measured or assessed.

There are many loud voices in our day, with each confidently—but often to our detriment—claiming to know the best course of action for our lives. Talk show hosts, activists, politicians, university professors, and religious leaders of various faiths all claim to know what's best for us. How confusing life can get! Sometimes we don't know which way is up. All too often, we find ourselves returning to the same desolate location we passed some time back. Talk about frustration! We would do well to realize that one voice alone stands true above all others, enabling us to find our bearings amidst the confusion.

Regardless of what our circumstances appear to be telling us, God's promises put everything into perspective. The great heroes of the faith understood these things. In following their examples, we can never find better points of reference in barren seasons than the promises given by the faithful and sovereign King of the Universe. No matter how much the terrain of this world may shift, or how heated the battles of our lives become, our Father's word stands as an immovable mountain towering over every desolate landscape.

Your current circumstances might be screaming with negativity and hopelessness. All that surrounds you may seem to indicate that God is absent or uncaring. You may feel lost in confusion over what's right and what's wrong. But God is our rock! We can trust His promises for guidance because each one serves as an expression of His faithful character.

As an example, consider the situation of an employee who is struggling with envy as he or she sees company executives unjustly padding their portfolios. Unfair? Absolutely. But is God absent? Not necessarily. This same individual cracks open the Bible to read the following passages:

> *Refrain from anger, and forsake wrath!*
> *Fret not yourself; it tends only to evil.*
> *For the evildoers shall be cut off,*
> *but those who wait for the LORD shall inherit the land.* Psalms 37:8-9 (ESV)

> *The name of the LORD is a strong tower;*
> *the righteous man runs into it and is safe.*
> *A rich man's wealth is his strong city,*
> *and like a high wall in his imagination.* Proverbs 18:10-11 (ESV)

> *Keep your life free from love of money, and be content with what you have, for he has said, "I will never leave you nor forsake you."* Hebrews 13:5 (ESV)

Can you feel it happening? In pondering these passages, we begin to gain God's perspective of the situation. Before, our hearts were growing cold and bitter, but now we are beginning to see that the unjust are the ones to be pitied. We now sense a quiet, but growing confidence that one day God will call every greedy person into account, and the consequences will not be pleasant! The person who cheats others—thinking that an unjust accumulation of wealth will provide shelter from future storms—builds nothing more than an imaginary fortress in vaporous clouds.

If you are faithfully serving God with integrity, seeking to honor Him in all of your ways, then you can rest assured that you are the one who stands secure. His favor will cover and protect you. He will never leave or forsake you. If you are faithful and patient, on a day certain to come, you will receive an eternal inheritance that makes their accumulation of wealth look like greenish mold on stale bread.

I have used the example of applying scriptural promises to gain a godly perspective to the issue of finances, but the principle is by no means limited to money. Like Joshua (and many others), we, too, can enter every battle with total confidence because of our Father's steadfast promise that He will never abandon us in our time of need. Let us identify and lay hold of the rock-solid promises of God as spiritual benchmarks so that we may successfully navigate the wilderness terrain before us.

PROBING QUESTIONS
What makes God's promises trustworthy?

Can you think of a time in your life when a promise of God helped to guide you through a wilderness experience?

What promise(s) do you cherish most in your current season?

ACTION STEP
Find and write out three promises from the Scriptures that apply to your current struggles. You can use Appendix I as a starting point if needed.

CLOSING PRAYER
Father, I thank You for Your rock-solid promises. Please help me to lay hold of those promises that I need for this season of my life.

FURTHER READING
Psalms 37:1-29; Hebrews 6:10-20; 2 Peter 1-11

CHAPTER TWENTY-FIVE
WILDERNESS OF OBSCURITY

Just as water ever seeks and fills the lowest place, so the moment God finds you abased and empty, His glory and power flow in.
—Andrew Murray, pastor and author

Again, the devil took him to a very high mountain and showed him all the kingdoms of the world and their glory. And he said to him, "All these I will give you, if you will fall down and worship me." Then Jesus said to him, "Be gone, Satan! For it is written,
'You shall worship the Lord your God
and him only shall you serve.'"
Then the devil left him, and behold, angels came and were ministering to him.

MATTHEW 4:8-11 (ESV)

Until I understood the significance of identity, I could never fully grasp the scope of the devil's scheme to tempt Jesus in the wilderness. I am sure there is more to be learned about the matter, but one thing I now understand: each of the three temptations was significant— and very powerful. The Son of God had gone from being the focal point of worship in heaven to total obscurity in the wilderness. For thirty years Jesus had walked this earth with only minimal attention. Satan was now offering Him the potential for glory without having to experience the pain and humiliation of the cross.

Jesus succeeded where all other humans had failed! He humbled Himself completely, honored the Father above all, and never attempted to grab glory for Himself. The only person to walk this earth who was truly worthy of glory willingly embraced a long season of obscurity.

The human heart ever craves glory and significance. Whether from a single individual, or from a massive crowd, we incessantly hunger to be validated. This "glory-quest" is so deeply ingrained in our hearts that we find it nearly impossible to eradicate. From a little boy running with all the speed he can muster to gain approval from his father, to a lonely woman sacrificing her dignity for the affirmation of a man, to grown men wearing tights and destroying their bodies to win a championship ring, glory is one of the most powerful motivating forces known to humankind. Our desire for significance colors every aspect of life; thus, every quest for eternal glory must, by necessity, involve some type of a journey through obscurity.

I have tasted my share of obscurity and, initially, it was all rather painful. How dare my girlfriend fail to mention my name in her testimony of God's blessings! Looking back, I can now see that my heart was overflowing with stupid human pride. Thankfully, she married me in spite of my issues!

Every wilderness experience, it seems, is tailored to something that God seeks to accomplish in an individual's heart. The trail of life often winds through lonely, shadow-filled valleys devoid of human applause. It is here that our carnal quests for human glory must meet their end. Only then will our Lord be fully honored.

We would be foolish to think that all who serve God are inspired by love alone. More often than not, our motives are mixed. A pastor may pour out his heart in a message, praying for the Holy Spirit to transform his listeners, but if they do not respond as expected, he will likely take it personally. An administrator may work tirelessly to put together a successful conference, but if her name isn't mentioned in the accolades, there is a good chance she will fly into anger, or sulk into depression. While such a mixture of motives is entirely natural, it can also prove deadly. Truly fruitful service can be motivated only by an *other-centered* love—the purity of which is often forged in the wilderness.

Moses fled to the wilderness. Having once seen himself as a mighty deliverer, he emerged a meek servant of God, the Bible calling him the most humble man on earth (Numbers 12:3). What began as a failure due to motives tainted with self-centered visions of grandeur, eventually morphed (over a period of forty years) into a powerful mission through God's supernatural grace!

Many a Christian leader has built a ministry in the name of God, but with an underlying motivation of personal glory. Because so much attention is given to souls to save and buildings to erect, impure motives can easily be ignored. Soon after a ministry has been successfully established, however, the fruit of pride surfaces in the forms of self-centeredness and a compulsion to control. The same drive that pushes a person to work so hard to establish a ministry can, in turn, give birth to spiritual termites that consume its very foundations.

Having been created in the image of God, each of us is wired for glory. But kingdom glory is of a very different sort than human glory, which is driven by a constant desire for self-elevation. Kingdom glory shines only as our fleshly tendencies are defeated, not exalted. When we forgive those who have callously injured us, God's glory shines. When we pray for heaven to bless what we view as a competing ministry, God's glory shines. When, in the midst of painful circumstances, we thank our Lord for His goodness, God's glory shines.

Rarely will the world take note of the obscure individual immersed in kingdom glory, but you can be sure that heaven's attention is captivated by every act of humble love. Wise Christians understand these things and are content to faithfully serve their Lord as they traverse the *Wilderness of Obscurity*. They genuinely do not care if glory and honor ever come through human accolades. If, however, they are somehow blessed to see a fruitful harvest from their labors, the wilderness will have prepared their hearts so that visible success does not result in a fatal curse.

PROBING QUESTIONS
Why do you think that humans so strongly pursue glory?

What are some of the efforts you personally have made in order to find significance?

How does human pride conflict with the advance of God's kingdom?

ACTION STEP
Prayerfully identify one or two areas of your life where you are currently seeking human glory. Surrender these desires to God, confessing any pride that might be coloring your actions.

CLOSING PRAYER
God of heaven, You alone are worthy of glory. Please purify my motives. May Your true glory never fail to shine through my life!

FURTHER READING
Proverbs 25:27; John 5:41-44; Acts 7:17-36; Philippians 2:5-11

CHAPTER TWENTY-SIX
WILDERNESS DEATH MARCH

If there be, therefore, perpetual failure in your life, it cannot arise from any weakness or impotence in the Mighty God; but from some failure on your part. That failure may probably be discovered in one of three hiding places—imperfect surrender, deficient faith, or neglected communion. But when the intention of the soul is right with God, without doubt He will save.

–F.B. Meyer, pastor and author

Today, if you hear his voice,
do not harden your hearts, as at Meribah,
as on the day at Massah in the wilderness,
when your fathers put me to the test
and put me to the proof, though they had seen my work.
For forty years I loathed that generation
and said, "They are a people who go astray in their heart,
and they have not known my ways."
Therefore I swore in my wrath,
"They shall not enter my rest."

PSALMS 95:7B-11 (ESV)

"For forty years I loathed that generation . . ." If ever there were a part of the Bible that I would not want to refer to me, this would be it! Stubborn and unbelieving, that wilderness generation of Israelites refused to trust and obey God—in spite of seeing His miraculous hand repeatedly work on their behalf. What would it take to change their attitudes? Nothing short of death.

Death marches have not been uncommon throughout the course of history; conquering powers frequently oppresses their captives in twisted celebration of the spoils of war. Painfully trudging over long distances, often in chains and with little food or water, far too many have died due to malnourishment and disease. But Israel's wilderness walk serves as a historical anomaly. God met their needs whenever necessary, and usually in miraculous ways. Time and time again, heaven sent a message of faithful love—often inked in dramatic fashion. Still, they refused to believe, bringing upon their own heads distain and death.

We prefer not to admit that we are born with a stubborn, prideful, and unbelieving nature—one that ever seeks to dominate not only our own lives, but all that surrounds us. Traumatic events further accentuate the unhealthy tendencies of a domineering nature to the point where the need to be in control becomes an all-consuming compulsion.

Looking back, the constant replay of well-worn mental reruns, and the immersion of quiet moments into swamps of regret, can be forms of control seeking as we vainly attempt to rewrite the past according to our wishes. Looking forward, we are drawn to secretly read our horoscopes, hoping that the stars will provide a cryptic message for a better tomorrow. Anxiety and depression then enter the picture as we grasp just how much in this world lies beyond the boundaries of our control.

Truth must be merciful, but real love never coddles sinful tendencies. Our old, fallen natures cannot be coaxed or redirected; the only path to freedom comes by killing what the Bible calls "the old man" (see Romans 6:5-7). I speak not of a physical death, such as suicide, but of death to our self-will in the form of spiritual surrender. We never fully experience new life in Christ without first dying to our old ways.

Those who embrace only the happy parts of Christianity will be sorely disappointed to learn that God fully intends a wilderness experience to be a "death march"—the most difficult struggle any of us will ever face—for the selfish will. We want what we want. There is just no getting around that reality. It should come as no surprise, then, that through the course of our journeys we will encounter problems and obstacles that cause the old nature to rear its head in selfishness, rebellion, and fear. Only one response to such situations will enable us to abide in the peace-filled life of God—an unconditional surrender to His will.

The call of any Christian is to follow in the footsteps of Christ. By both word and deed, Jesus demonstrated that He came seeking to do the Father's will and not His own. The greatest all-time victory over the will, and the one that stands in complete antithesis to ancient Israel's miserable failure, took place in the garden of Gethsemane as the magnificent Christ surrendered Himself fully to the heavenly Father's will. If ever someone paid the price of self-denial in the midst of unbearable pain, it was Jesus!

How many of our vices are little more than the products of stubborn, unbelieving hearts? Unbelief and the stubborn will—the two feed off of one another like drunken criminals. Failing to believe in God, we grow more and more set in our prideful ways. And the more established our self-willed patterns become, the less likely we are to exercise any type of meaningful faith toward Him who is always faithful.

Of course, any professing Christian can attempt to follow his or her own will in the name of God, but such an approach doesn't work very well. An unsurrendered life equates to a miserable existence. Try as we will, we have no other viable option but to yield ourselves entirely to God's good plans and purposes.

There was a time when I desperately wanted to jump into ministry as a career, but circumstances beyond my control would not allow it. If ever I had an opportunity to fake doing the will of God, it was then. My desire for ministry was indeed noble and, from a distance, I would have been seen as sacrificially pursuing God's plans and purposes. I could not, however, continue my life's journey without fully surrendering even my good desires. What was it that finally enabled me to let go of what I wanted?—only the confidence that I could entrust my entire future into the hands of my loving Father who has planned for me a hope-filled tomorrow. When the time was right, and when my heart's desires had been conformed to His will, He finally released me from my job in the lab into the fullness of my calling. Little did I know then how important it was that my heart had been prepared through that dead end job!

How long should a wilderness season last? It is not within our power to set such a timetable. However, I can say with confidence that such a season will be unduly extended as long as a person's will continues to diverge from God's. The old, stubborn, unbelieving nature must be laid to rest in the barren landscape of the wilderness. Only then will God's lasting peace become reality.

PROBING QUESTIONS
How can the desire/need to be in control lead to anxiety and depression?

Why was Christ's surrender of His will in the garden of Gethsemane such a victorious moment in history?

How does unbelief hinder a person from fully surrendering his or her will to God?

ACTION STEP
If you have never fully surrendered your will to God, it begins with a simple but sincere prayer. If you are unwilling, ask Him to help you to become willing.

CLOSING PRAYER
Lord, I choose to surrender my life, my relationships, and my future completely to You. Please grant me the grace to peacefully live out this reality.

FURTHER READING
Matthew 26:36-42; Luke 9:23-25; Romans 6:1-11; Hebrews 3

STAGE THREE
FINDING REST, PURPOSE, AND SECURITY IN DESOLATE PLACES

Where does your security lie? Is God your refuge, your hiding place, your stronghold, your shepherd, your counselor, your friend, your redeemer, your saviour, your guide? If He is, you don't need to search any further for security.

–Elisabeth Elliot, author and speaker

―――――――――

**For a child will be born to us, a son will be given to us;
And the government will rest on His shoulders;
And His name will be called Wonderful Counselor, Mighty God,
Eternal Father, Prince of Peace.
There will be no end to the increase of His government or of peace,
On the throne of David and over his kingdom,
To establish it and to uphold it with justice and righteousness
From then on and forevermore.
The zeal of the LORD of hosts will accomplish this.**

ISAIAH 9:6-7 (NASB)

―――――――――

Nothing in this world is truly secure. Through Stage Three of our journey, we will seek to lay hold of the rest and security that can be found only through Jesus Christ.

CHAPTER TWENTY-SEVEN
THE MERCY OF FAILURE

Success is on the same road as failure; success is just a little further down the road.

–Jack Hyles, pastor and author

Moses was a very humble man, more so than any man on the face of the earth.

NUMBERS 12:3 (HCSB)

Have you ever met someone who always seemed to succeed with ease? When it came to hunting and fishing, Amazing George was the man. George was so good at fishing that we often found ourselves in awe; thus, we gave him the moniker, "Amazing George"—although we never called him that to his face because George was also in the habit of constantly reminding us of his success!

I, on the other hand, was a trout fisherman wannabe. I have always loved being on the water, but at that point in my life, stream fishing was mostly a lesson in futility. As a result, even being around George became painful at times. Such feelings made it especially difficult to obey God when we sensed Him leading us to invite George to our annual trout fishing camp experience.

At one point during the weekend, I found myself fishing a nice looking hole on Bald Eagle Creek but—not surprisingly—with no success. George meandered down the stream, asked if I minded if he fished the hole, and cast his line into the water before I had a chance to answer. Bang! Bang! Within just a few minutes, George had two strikes and landed both fish. He then continued downstream while I stood there frustrated, shaking my head in disbelief.

Later that weekend, while on Fishing Creek, I somehow managed to hook a nice-sized rainbow trout and brought to within a few feet of my boots. The feeling was exhilarating—landing that trophy would shine at least a little glory in my direction! Having minimal experience with larger fish, however, I could not bring it into my net. My heart sank as the rainbow broke free and swam back into the current. Dejected, I put more bait on my hook and cast it out to the same spot in the river. Do you know what happened? Exactly the same thing! I hooked that rainbow and lost it at my boots again! The only difference was that my heart sank a little further into my stomach the second time around. I dreaded the thought of facing George.

I could have chosen to remain silent and hide my failure, rehearsing in my mind how life wasn't fair—how I, as a faithful servant of God, always seemed to come up short while others around me succeeded. But I choose another course of action—the high (or low, depending on one's perspective) road of humility. I swallowed my pride and told the story to George, asking what I should have done differently. After briefly chiding me for my stupidity, George explained the need to keep my rod tip high and my line free of slack. Taking his instructions to heart, I tucked them in the back of my mind for future use.

The following spring we returned to what I now thought of as "Lost Rainbow River", but this time I had the most successful trout fishing experience of my entire life! With all that I had learned from George, I landed three beautiful browns that day, in addition to several others. That was when I learned that failure, when accompanied by faith and humility, is the springboard to future success.

No one likes to fail. I've never met a little boy whose vision for life was to become a failure. Imagine Aunt Betty pinching her nephew's little cheeks. "Johnny, what do you want to be when you grow up?" "Aunt Betty, I really want to be a *failure* when I get big!"

But aside from the damage to the human ego, is failure really as bad as we make it to be? Is it possible that there might be long-term benefits to falling short? Failure, in a very real way, puts us in our place. The desire for glory is innate to human nature, and, though short-lived, with a sense of satisfaction and superiority we will milk every ounce of glory for all it's worth. It is all very superficial, however, for in the grand scheme of eternity, trout fishing (and just about every other human pursuit) means absolutely nothing. Humility before God, on the other hand, has powerful ramifications both in this age and in the age to come.

The Bible tells us that Moses was the most humble man in all the earth. Why do you think that was? He had lived for forty years on top of the world, immersed in the wealth and splendor of the royal family of the greatest kingdom on earth. Then, by his own strength, Moses tried to deliver his people, failing miserably in the process. How did he spend the next forty years of his life? On the backside of the desert as a "stinking" shepherd. (I say "stinking" not because I think poorly of shepherds, but because shepherding was despised by the Egyptians as being far below their standards of significance.) The humility worked into Moses's heart during his wilderness experience led him to become one of the most highly esteemed men in all of Scripture.

We can find a tangible connection between sports, academics, morality, and just about any other area of life that involves measuring up to standards of perfection. Failure opens our eyes to our need for something—or Someone—outside of ourselves, giving us a chance to align our lives with the dynamics of God's eternal kingdom. It is an opportunity that a perpetually successful person will probably never have. Like it or not, our failures can sometimes be powerful expressions of God's mercy.

Most unwanted wilderness experiences are beset by nagging feelings of inadequacy, if not by failure itself. But failure need not have the last word! When navigated wisely, our shortcomings will effectively instill the godly (and necessary) virtue of meekness. The humility and faith forged through a wilderness experience will always pave a powerful pathway to true and lasting glory.

PROBING QUESTIONS
Why is failure so painful for us?

Can you think of a time when an initial failure produced a long-term blessing in your life?

How is failure, when accompanied by faith and humility, the springboard for future success?

ACTION STEP
Call to mind a painful time when you failed miserably—one that perhaps still plagues you. Ask God to show you how that failure might actually be to your benefit.

CLOSING PRAYER
My Father, I thank You that my value in Your eyes is not dependent upon my ability to succeed in this world. Please grant me the grace to humbly learn from my failures.

FURTHER READING
Luke 22:54-62; Acts 2:14, 2:41, 3:12, 4:4, 7:17-30; 1 Corinthians 15:1-11

CHAPTER TWENTY-EIGHT
"WHAT ABOUT ME?"

Love is the overflow of joy in God! It is not duty for duty's sake, or right for right's sake. . . . It is first a deeply satisfying experience of the fullness of God's grace, and then a doubly satisfying experience of sharing that grace with another person.

–John Piper, pastor and author

The next day Moses sat to judge the people, and the people stood around Moses from morning till evening. . . . Moses' father-in-law said to him, "What you are doing is not good. You and the people with you will certainly wear yourselves out, for the thing is too heavy for you. You are not able to do it alone."

EXODUS 18:13, 17-18 (ESV)

Service to others can sometimes seem like a wilderness in its own right. The days are long, things don't always go well (to put it mildly), and there are seasons when no one seems to appreciate our efforts. All too often, we find ourselves asking, *What About Me? Is anybody going to care for my needs?*

The answer, which may be surprising, is both "yes" and "no." Yes, our God will surely care for our needs as we make sacrifices in loving obedience to Him, but those sacrifices must be aligned with God's design for our lives. God called Moses to lead His people, but Moses needed wisdom to lead in such a way that he didn't destroy himself. Thankfully, his father-in-law (Jethro) was there to offer some timely advice. How I wish there were more people like Jethro in this world!

Unfortunately, people like Jethro are far too few. The chances that others will make a deliberate effort to ensure our spiritual and familial well-being are sometimes very slim. It then falls upon our own shoulders to pursue a walk with God and to ensure that the needs of our families are met.

"What About Me?" is a question we must ask ourselves with regard to knowing God and caring for our families. Are we deliberately pursuing our Lord and Savior above all else? Are we spending time in His word and in prayer? Are we following the example of Jesus by periodically stepping away from the responsibilities of life to seek our heavenly Father? Are we meeting the needs of our spouses and children in the midst of what appear to be overwhelming needs? Are we serving as a part of a ministry team rather than attempting to carry a multitude of the burdens on our own shoulders? Only as we focus on doing life and ministry according to God's design will He answer all of the other *"What About Me?"* needs.

Let's not fool ourselves into thinking that we can effectively serve God apart from God. We have nothing of real value to offer others that we aren't getting first from the throne of heaven. This means that deliberately carving out personal and family time is one of the most unselfish things we can do. Unfortunately for us, such an approach to life and ministry is not exactly what one might call *conscience-friendly*. Service motivated by love is redemptive. In contrast, a heart driven by guilt will never fail to bear corrupt fruit.

I saw one of the most striking examples of this struggle during my campus ministry years. We were each responsible for raising our own salaries, feeling as though a sacred trust had been given to us by those giving sacrificially to support our ministry efforts. Accordingly, we all felt the pressure to work 24/7. Time away from ministry—although essential to our well-being—was often plagued by an underlying sense of guilt. Add to the mix the unreasonable expectations of a few unhappy people, and the guilt cocktail was complete.

Personally, I was privileged to work with college students who genuinely appreciated our efforts and rarely tried to take thoughtless advantage of our family. Such is not always the case when it comes to Christian ministry. (Is it really on anybody's agenda to work long, hard hours with little appreciation and often painfully low pay?) In an ideal world, those around us would have an eye out for our personal needs. Thankfully, some people in ministry are blessed to be surrounded by others who express genuine concern for their well-being. All too often, however, those receiving ministry feel a sense of entitlement, that somehow they deserve what others are giving. Some individuals are so self-absorbed that they give little or no thought about the welfare of the ones who sacrificially serve. Worse still, a ministry can be run like a cold, hard business where the bottom line is the size of a meeting, or the number of decisions made for Christ. Current usefulness is all that seems to matter.

Doing things for God (and others) is not equivalent to walking with God; truly effective ministry is always a matter of spiritual overflow. Our heavenly Father never calls us to bankrupt our souls to serve others, but to give out of the abundance that flows from a personal relationship with Him. And if we neglect and destroy our families, our Christian witness is seriously undermined.

It falls to us to overcome internal voices of guilt and external voices of demand in order to set appropriate boundaries in our lives and ministries. We are all called to serve God, but none of us has the infinite capacity of the Holy Spirit. Yes, we want to give sacrificially for the benefit of others, but giving must also be wise. As evidenced by the example of Christ, intentionally developing leaders and periodically pulling away from the crowds to pursue our Father are two of the best things we can do for those we serve. Further still, sensitivity to the needs of a spouse and children will not only ensure their favorable view of the Christian faith, but also enable us to continue to serve from a healthy foundation.

"What About Me?" If we answer this question according to God's design, He will answer all of the other *"What About Me?"* needs.

PROBING QUESTIONS
Why must we be deliberate to labor *wisely* for God?

What are some of the reasons we might carry the burdens of labor by ourselves?

What are we offering people if we are not serving through an overflow of God's grace?

ACTION STEP
If you are serving in ministry, are you protecting vital relationships? If you are currently receiving ministry, have you discussed appropriate boundaries with those who are serving you? Take a survey of your life and write out some of the boundaries that you need to put in place.

CLOSING PRAYER
Lord, help me to understand human limitations in light of Your ability. Teach me to serve others from the overflow of my relationship with You.

FURTHER READING
Matthew 14:22-23; 1 Timothy 3:1-7; 2 Timothy 2:2; Revelation 2:1-7

CHAPTER TWENTY-NINE
THE EPIC BATTLE FOR CONTROL

One for the Dark Lord on his dark throne
In the Land of Mordor where the Shadows lie.
One Ring to rule them all, One Ring to find them,
One Ring to bring them all and in the darkness bind them.
                    —from *The Lord of the Rings* by J.R.R. Tolkien

---

The LORD God took the man and placed him in the garden of Eden to work it and watch over it. And the LORD God commanded the man, "You are free to eat from any tree of the garden, but you must not eat from the tree of the knowledge of good and evil, for on the day you eat from it, you will certainly die."

GENESIS 2:15-17 (HCSB)

Two things were common in the area of western Pennsylvania where I grew up: farms and coal mines. One did not need to travel far from town to find a herd of cows leisurely grazing in a field. Little did they realize that the fences surrounding them served as signs of their impending doom. The day would arrive soon enough for the butcher to do his deadly work.

Abandoned coal mines were less abundant, but still easy to find—especially by curious teens. On one occasion, some friends and I discovered an abandoned mine behind my Uncle Johnny's house. Carved into the side of a hill, we could have walked right into the mine shaft. Although tempted to do so, enough wisdom had somehow seeped into our teenage male brains to prevent us from going further. Old coal mines have unstable ceilings—if not for a brief moment of good judgment, writing this book would have been nothing more than unfulfilled potential!

Thankfully, most of the abandoned mine shafts had fences. Those boundaries, however, served a very different purpose than the ones around the cow pastures; rather than keeping captives, they were intended only to keep us safe. Such is the nature of God's only commandment in the garden of Eden. Its sole purpose was to keep the inhabitants of the garden safe from harm. Why the tree of the knowledge of good and evil was there to begin with is a topic for another work. What we need to understand in our current context is that some boundaries are necessary for our protection.

God alone is free to do whatever He wants; His only boundaries are self-imposed. Humans, on the other hand, are finite creatures. If we transgress the oxygen boundary, for example, we suffocate. If we attempt to escape gravity, we may fall to our deaths. If we go without sleep for any length of time, we begin to pay a steep price. Boundaries are necessary for our well-being. Any difficult wilderness journey will become all the more grievous if we transgress these God-given lines.

Fallen angels (demons) possess an incessant lust for power that finds fulfillment only through the domination of others. On the contrary, God does not need to directly control humans (or demons for that matter) in order to accomplish His will on earth. Unfortunately, because Adam and Eve obeyed the voice of the serpent rather than God's, they and their descendants inherited the same controlling tendencies of Satan and his demons. Humans and demons, being limited in wisdom, power, and authority, must always seek to control all that surrounds them in order to get what they want. More problematic still, is the fact that in seeking to have our own way, humans play into Satan's hands, serving only as naïve pawns in his destructive game.

Through his imaginative fantasy, *The Lord of the Rings*, J.R.R. Tolkien brilliantly developed a host of biblical themes in creative form. Real life, the sage Tolkien understood, is but an *Epic Battle for Control* that plays itself out in unfamiliar wilderness territory. And our options, it seems, are only two. We either wisely surrender our human desires to the will of God, or we seek control for ourselves, foolishly playing into Satan's schemes. To put it into biblical language, we fully embrace God's kingdom rule, or we become hapless and disposable subjects in the kingdom of darkness.

Why do we need boundaries? Not to constrain us, but to keep us safe within the territory of God's kingdom. No matter what area of life we consider, *controlling spirits* of one form or another will always arise as they seek to dominate and destroy. A primary responsibility of every Christian, then, is to live and lead in such a way as to facilitate the advance of God's kingdom—to the exclusion of that which seeks to control. Those who try to control the circumstances of their lives and the people around them will soon find themselves isolated from His loving presence.

Rest, I believe, serves as an excellent example to illustrate the importance of healthy boundaries. In the Old Covenant, God commanded clear times of Sabbath rest—times when His people were compelled to lay down their labors and trust Him to care for their needs. Through the process, there was no question who was and who wasn't God. And although we are no longer bound by the Mosaic Law, the value of a physical Sabbath still rings true.

Much of my own life revolves around an effort to advance God's kingdom. I have learned, however, that if I do not periodically lay down my work to take seasons of rest, I soon begin to sink my "claws of ownership" into what actually belongs to God. How easy it is for those of us in Christian leadership to wrestle for control, and to do so in the name of Christ!

Rest is but one of many examples we could highlight, but regardless of which arena of life is addressed, the principle remains the same. The battle is deceptive, ferocious, and unpleasant. We, therefore, must be wise and vigilant to draw boundary lines to protect ourselves, our families, and our ministries from the controlling tendencies of man and devil.

PROBING QUESTIONS

What is the difference between a protective boundary and a boundary that holds one captive?

Why is it that those who seek to be in control foolishly play into Satan's hands?

Are there areas of your life in which you are seeking your own will in the name of God's?

ACTION STEP

Identify an area or two of your life in which clearer boundaries need to be drawn in order to protect God's people and advance His kingdom. Prayerfully map out those boundaries.

CLOSING PRAYER

Dear God, please grant me the wisdom and courage to live in such a way that I let go of control and advance only Your kingdom.

FURTHER READING

Exodus 31:12-17; Matthew 6:9-15; Revelation 11:15-18

CHAPTER THIRTY
BIGGER, BETTER, MORE?

Any darn fool can make something complex; it takes a genius to make something simple.

–Pete Seeger, folk singer

Immediately He made the disciples get into the boat and go ahead of Him to the other side, while He sent the crowds away. After He had sent the crowds away, He went up on the mountain by Himself to pray; and when it was evening, He was there alone.

MATTHEW 14:22-23 (NASB)

People like Tim, the mechanic, are a rarity these days. An older guy with a kind, humble heart, Tim won't tackle anything that's very complicated, choosing to limit his work to routine types of automotive maintenance. The operation is relatively low-tech, but his prices are reasonable.

Not long ago, I called Tim to schedule an oil change. My life was busy and so I was thankful that he could take the car in immediately. As I pulled into the parking lot, a lack of other vehicles caught my attention. A little concerned that his business was floundering, I asked Tim how it was going. That particular summer day was indeed slow, but he assured me that overall his business was steady. Tim explained that he didn't have a huge clientele because he preferred not to tackle too many repairs on a given day. In other words, Tim is quite content with a steady but consistent income—even though it might not be all that large.

Our *Bigger, Better, More* culture would despise Tim's modest approach. I suspect, however, that Tim has something up on the rest of the world. Day-to-day peace is as big a part of Tim's quality of life as is the ability to grow his business, or to buy (and accumulate) possessions. Sadly, the *Bigger, Better, More* mentality is now ingrained in our society to the point that anything less strikes us as odd.

A significant drawback of prosperity is the amount of unnecessary stuff that people tend to accumulate. More stuff means more time, effort, and money to care for what we own, often at the expense of our spiritual vitality. No rule states that material and spiritual prosperity must conflict with one another, but they often do because it is so difficult to navigate both worlds effectively. The result is that many who prosper financially suffer from the disease of chronic spiritual dryness. Their wilderness may be beautifully decorated, but it is spiritually parched nonetheless.

Over the years, I have noticed a ministry trend toward more activity and less prayer. This tendency seems to be as true for Christian leaders as for the average believer. Is it because we don't care? Not at all. Simply put, prayer takes time and a certain measure of stillness. When life is busy, prayer is one of the first activities to be neglected. Unavoidably, a person's walk with God will suffer when a vital prayer life is lacking.

While I believe that specific times of retreat are needed to help us refocus, adjustments in how we do life may also be necessary. Such changes, however, are not easily made. Life's demands don't mysteriously vaporize because we seek simplicity, and, unless we choose an isolated existence devoid of influence on others, a certain measure of complication is unavoidable. Ministry to others will always make our lives *more* complicated—all the more reason for us to take practical steps to simplify our personal lives.

Pruning is a concept that doesn't make a lot of natural sense apart from an agricultural perspective. Yes, we understand the need to cut away the "dead wood"—those activities that take away from the quality of our lives. Watching long hours of television, for example, has never done much good for anybody.

Further still, even an overabundance of good can be bad. My blueberry bushes provide an excellent example. When the branches become too numerous, the size and quality of the berries suffer. I have learned firsthand the importance of trudging out to the garden in the dead of winter to cut off not only the dead branches, but some living ones as well. Sweet, beautiful berries are the result; and, trust me, they aren't lacking in number!

In my own warped way, I sometimes wonder how my berry bushes feel when I prune them. I'm the one who has cared for these plants since they were small seedlings. They are accustomed to me covering their roots with mulch, picking off Japanese beetles, and providing water in dry weather. But on one cold day each year, I cut off some of their arms. I can sometimes picture a bush shouting, "Ouch! Why are you hurting me? Can't you see that I am trying to grow?"

Pruning, you see, is another activity that is not conscience-friendly. There are so many needs across the globe that we often feel obligated to try to meet them all. Isn't that, after all, what good Christians do? Such a mindset either paralyzes us because we are overwhelmed by the multitude of needs we can't possibly meet, or burns us out through our attempts to do too much. The truth be told—the burdens of this world fall on Christ's shoulders and not ours. Our call is to walk with Him, staying closely connected to our Lord and Savior in an abiding relationship. As the head of the church, He will direct the various expressions of His body to meet the needs that surround us. If all professing Christians stayed connected to God and submitted to His will, our world would be a much better place. I have never been an advocate of inactivity, but I also understand that to attempt to do everything is to do nothing well.

When it comes to simplicity, I don't think we can find a better example than Jesus. He voluntarily limited His possessions, He pruned His following when false disciples began to gather, and He persistently went off by Himself to spend time with the Father. May our Lord give us the wisdom and courage to follow in His steps!

PROBING QUESTIONS

What is behind our tendency to accumulate stuff?

How does this impact our spiritual vitality?

Why do we so often put service and activity before a personal relationship with God?

ACTION STEP

Take some time to look at your calendar, listing the activities and obligations that fill your life. Identify those things that are truly necessary, prayerfully developing a plan to eliminate activities you don't need to be doing (and things you don't need to own). Please be considerate of others as you make any necessary changes.

CLOSING PRAYER

Dear Jesus, please grant me the wisdom to simplify my life in this complicated world!

FURTHER READING

Deuteronomy 8; Luke 10:38-42; John 15:1-8

CHAPTER THIRTY-ONE
GOD'S SABBATH REST

*The branch of the vine does not worry, and toil, and rush here to
seek for sunshine, and there to find rain. No; it rests in union and
communion with the vine; and at the right time, and in the right
way, is the right fruit found on it. Let us so abide in the Lord Jesus.*
    —Hudson Taylor, missionary to inland China

**While the Israelites were in the wilderness, they found a
man gathering wood on the Sabbath day. Those who found
him gathering wood brought him to Moses, Aaron, and the
entire community. They placed him in custody because it
had not been decided what should be done to him. Then
the LORD told Moses, "The man is to be put to death. The
entire community is to stone him outside the camp." So
the entire community brought him outside the camp and
stoned him to death, as the LORD had commanded Moses.**
NUMBERS 15:32-36 (HCSB)

Let's be honest—there were some terribly unpleasant (and probably
confusing) aspects of the ancient Israelite's journey through the
wilderness. We know that honoring the Sabbath was one of the Ten
Commandments, but the judgment meted out on this poor soul
appears, at first glance, to be extreme and unfair.

In order to get a proper perspective on this event, three
important considerations must be taken into account. First, with
the giving of the Ten Commandments, the nation of Israel found
itself under a standard of law. Law breeds judgment, and so a

harsh penalty was to be expected. Second, the force of this man's punishment communicates the life and death importance of living in accordance with God's design. Finally, this is another example of an Old Testament *type* foreshadowing a greater New Testament truth.

The Old Covenant Sabbath day provides a powerful picture of the New Covenant plan of salvation through faith in Jesus Christ. Letting go of our compulsive need to measure up to various standards of perfection frees us from impossible burdens, bringing much needed rest to our souls. The warning is strikingly clear: any person who attempts to work for his or her salvation will face the penalty of eternal death—an existence devoid of rest. If this appears to be extreme, it may be helpful to point out that salvation by good works would allow human pride to enter heaven. Such pride is what unleashed all of the pain, suffering, and death that incessantly plague our planet.

Under the New Covenant, keeping a physical Sabbath day each week is no longer a legalistic requirement for God's people, yet the principle overflows with wisdom. Too often, we see non-stop work as virtuous—especially when our labors are in service to God. But if we use the term "workaholic", the connotation changes drastically. Effective labor for God can only be achieved as we spend time with our Father, resting in His presence and drawing upon His divine strength.

All too often, our wilderness seasons are complicated by a failure to obey biblical patterns of rest. God designed our world with a natural order of days, years, seasons, etc. Both mind and body need cycles of labor and rest in order to function properly, with our need for rest serving as a powerful reminder of our human frailty. We cannot do whatever we want whenever we want. In other words, we are not gods. Thus, it should come as no surprise that some essential elements of spiritual rest profoundly affect not only our souls, but our physical bodies as well.

Sleep is the most obvious type of rest and, of course, one of the most necessary. Life is demanding enough within itself, but a preoccupation with media will deceptively steal our sleep and contribute to an underlying sense of weariness. In addition, today's advances in technology often mean that we live in a constant state of distraction, which in turn creates a cumulative feeling of stress. Periodically turning off the TV, computer, or phone may do wonders in helping to renew both mind and body. Even when physically exhausted, Jesus often retreated for times of prayer to commune with His heavenly Father. During these invaluable times, Jesus drew strength from His Father and received guidance for His journey on earth.

Several other types of rest can help us to more effectively navigate a wilderness journey, ensuring that our hearts don't become dry and barren. I believe, however, that any plan for rest must be tailored to meet our individual needs and personalities. Getting out on the water to fish, for example, might have a very different effect for a pastor than for a professional fisherman. Mulling around the garden may be therapeutic to some, but a burdensome chore to others. To a stay-at-home mother with five kids, simply leaving the house alone for a few hours can do wonders. My advice is to find which types of rest benefit you most and to pursue those avenues.

While in the wilderness, Jesus practiced a less obvious form of rest we call "fasting". Fasting is vastly ignored and yet, it can have such a dynamic impact! Deliberately abstaining from food (or certain types of food) for a season gives our bodily organs time to rest, while providing additional time for prayer and Bible reading. Fasting may not make much sense to some of us, but its potential power is nothing short of profound.

It seems odd that we should have to labor to enter into rest (see Hebrews 4:11), but intentionality is essential as many necessary forms of rest do not come naturally. Life is a marathon, not a sprint. Learn to wisely abide in God's provision of rest and you may just find yourself flying!

PROBING QUESTIONS

What is the New Covenant lesson communicated through Numbers 15:32-36?

Why must many forms of rest be intentional on our part?

Why is rest often unfriendly to the human conscience?

ACTION STEP
What form of rest do you need the most but pursue the least? If needed, work out plans now to schedule some time to recharge.

CLOSING PRAYER
Heavenly Father, You rested after creation, not because You were tired, but to set an example for us to follow. Please grant me Your healthy perspective on rest, providing the time and ability for this need to be met in my life.

FURTHER READING
Genesis 2:1-3; Isaiah 58:6-14; Hebrews 4:1-11

CHAPTER THIRTY-TWO
ARE YOU WEARY AND HEAVY LADEN?

Abide in Me says Jesus. Cling to Me. Stick fast to Me. Live the life of close and intimate communion with Me. Get nearer to Me. Roll every burden on Me. Cast your whole weight on Me. Never let go your hold on Me for a moment. Be, as it were, rooted and planted in Me. Do this and I will never fail you. I will ever abide in you.
–J.C. Ryle, pastor and author

Lamech lived one hundred and eighty-two years, and became the father of a son. Now he called his name Noah, saying, "This one will give us rest from our work and from the toil of our hands arising from the ground which the LORD has cursed."

GENESIS 5:28-29 (NASB)

I can only begin to imagine the burdens that Noah would have been tempted to carry throughout the course of his life. We know from Genesis 6:5-6 that the wickedness of humankind was so great that God regretted creating the human race. For any godly person, simply living in such an evil environment would have been an immense burden within itself. God then commanded Noah to build the ark for the safe passage of his immediate family—his wife, his sons, and his sons' wives. No parents, grandparents, or cousins would be included. The massive, albeit lonely, building campaign was begun with the full knowledge that every person on earth apart from his small family would perish.

How daunting the work must have been! How heavy his concern for those around him! And yet, for dozens of years he continued the work in obedience to God. It is difficult to know if the passing of his father (Lamech) a few years before the flood was an added weight, or a relief—perhaps a measure of both. Noah's grandfather, Methuselah, died the year of the flood. We don't know if he perished in the deluge, or if he died a natural death before the flooding began. Regardless of the timing, what heaviness and pain Noah must have felt when the flooding rains began to fall!

These were by no means the sum total of Noah's concerns. Due to its size, construction of the ark would have presented significant difficulties. Further still, how was he to gather all of those animals and enough food to feed them for an unknown period of time? And what about closing the door of the ark? Who knows how many sleepless nights the poor guy spent trying to figure out how he would close that stupid door! In the end, God intervened and closed the door for him.

As it is with the birth of a baby, don't think for a minute that the sleepless nights ended when the flooding began. For over a year, all of the animals—some of which were nocturnal—needed to be tended. One can only imagine the overall effect of the experience on the ark's eight passengers—just keeping everyone happy in the midst of the damp, malodorous gloom would have presented a challenge comparable to building the ark!

The name *Noah* sounds similar to the Hebrew word for *rest*, and through his story we find yet another Old Testament illustration of a New Covenant truth. All of our burdens are to be cast upon God as He brings us safely through the destruction and wickedness around us. Don't be fooled into thinking that how we handle a sin-filled environment has little meaning—our response to such adversity matters a great deal.

It seems to me that most of us err toward being either irresponsible, or overly responsible. Those who are irresponsible undoubtedly will reap the negative consequences of their neglect, but the other extreme is unhealthy as well. Our natural tendencies toward controlling our lives, circumstances, and the people around us will lead us to carry burdens never intended for our shoulders. Such behavior may on the surface leave an appearance of sacrificial nobility, but it will bear the fruit of death nonetheless. By burdening our shoulders with weights we were never intended to carry, we exhaust ourselves both physically and spiritually.

Surrendering our loved ones into God's capable hands will benefit them much more than we realize. He loves them more perfectly than we ever could, and by relinquishing them into His wise care, we give Him the freedom to change their hearts and direct their steps. If we refuse to let go, we will hinder the Father from working in their lives. I can't begin to tell you how many women I have met who, after years of trying to convert their husbands, finally threw their hands up in the air and surrendered them fully to God, only to see those men come to Christ shortly thereafter.

We have no way of knowing how Noah handled the burdens he was tempted to carry, but we do know that our heavenly Father understands our struggles and that He sent Jesus as an answer to our needs. Isaiah prophesied that the government would "rest on His shoulders" and that He would be called the "Prince of Peace" (Isaiah 9:6). The connection between the two is profound! Letting go of control means rolling our burdens onto His broad, more-than-capable, and always willing shoulders. Taking time to surrender our responsibilities and cares to God each morning—and throughout the day for that matter—helps to facilitate the coming of God's life-giving kingdom, enabling us to labor from a foundation of peace and emotional rest.

Are You Weary and Heavy Laden? Whether we speak of the burdens of today or tomorrow, the weight of the load belongs to God. He will give us the grace we need to navigate desolate territory as we obediently surrender the weight of our concerns into His skillful hands.

PROBING QUESTIONS
Do you tend to be more irresponsible, or overly responsible?

What are some of the negative consequences of such tendencies?

Does surrendering a loved one to God mean that we stop praying, or that we abandon all sense of responsibility that we might have regarding that person? Why, or why not?

ACTION STEP
Are you usurping God's authority by trying to control a loved one(s) that you are concerned about? Get on your knees and fully surrender that person(s) to God.

CLOSING PRAYER
Father, You love the people in my life more than I do. Help me to know that and to believe that You will perfect Your work in their lives. I surrender control of myself and my loved ones fully to You. Please grant me the grace and wisdom I need to live out Your kingdom in a practical manner.

FURTHER READING
Isaiah 9:1-7; Matthew 11:28-30; 1 Peter 5:1-11; 1 John 5:1-3

CHAPTER THIRTY-THREE
THE WEIGHT OF TOMORROW

It is not the cares of today, but the cares of tomorrow, that weigh a man down. For the needs of today we have corresponding strength given. For the morrow we are told to trust. It is not ours yet. It is when tomorrow's burden is added to the burden of today that the weight is more than a man can bear.

–George McDonald, author and pastor

Abraham took the wood of the burnt offering and laid it on Isaac his son, and he took in his hand the fire and the knife. So the two of them walked on together. Isaac spoke to Abraham his father and said, "My father!" And he said, "Here I am, my son." And he said, "Behold, the fire and the wood, but where is the lamb for the burnt offering?" Abraham said, "God will provide for Himself the lamb for the burnt offering, my son." So the two of them walked on together. . . . Then Abraham raised his eyes and looked, and behold, behind him a ram caught in the thicket by his horns; and Abraham went and took the ram and offered him up for a burnt offering in the place of his son. Abraham called the name of that place The LORD Will Provide, as it is said to this day, "In the mount of the LORD it will be provided."

GENESIS 22:6-8, 13-14 (NASB)

Who knows what was going through Abraham's mind as he walked with his son toward the designated site of sacrifice? How surreal it must have felt! The same God who had brought Abraham a promised son through twenty-five years of trial and waiting was now calling him to sacrifice his beloved Isaac as a burnt offering. To make matters worse, the young man had to carry the wood for his own sacrificial fire! Abraham is the father of our faith for very good reason. Even though the scenario made no logical sense, he trusted that his covenant God would work everything out in the end—and He did.

At the young age of twenty-five, I became my "mother's father". Such a statement makes sense only to those who have cared for an elderly or ailing parent. My parents were fairly old when I arrived, somewhat unexpectedly. Later, just before I turned sixteen, my dad passed away after an extended illness. The addition of Mom's physical and emotional struggles made our difficult situation appear impossible. Not long after graduating from college, I was dealing with the same issues as seasoned people in their fifties and sixties who were looking after aging parents. Just thinking about the future saturated my soul with anxiety; I could not possibly see how everything was going to work out. But work out it did! God provided for our every need and my mother's last ten years of life were probably her most peaceful.

How much grief do we put ourselves (and others) through over fears that never come to pass? How much unnecessary weight do we attempt to carry through rigorous territory? Navigating the treacherous expanse of a wilderness experience is difficult enough within itself. Carrying *The Weight of Tomorrow* makes a successful outcome to the journey virtually impossible.

If you have ever been to a tractor pull, in addition to the deafening noise and acrid smoke polluting the air, you'll notice that the tractors pull a sled on which is mounted a system of weights. The further the tandem goes, the heavier the weights become until the huge wheels lose traction and the tractor bogs down. In a similar vein, our sense of exhaustion is multiplied as we carry not only the today's burdens, but those of tomorrow as well. God gives us grace to face the burdens of today only; tomorrow's needs belong to Him.

Why do we try to carry tomorrow's burdens? Simply put, the answer is *fear*. We don't believe that our heavenly Father will work things out in a favorable manner. We attempt to usurp control of what belongs to God; the foolish reasonings of our hearts convincing us that we can bring about a better outcome. It all sounds quite silly when we take the time to think about it, but those who have experienced considerable pain and hardship don't always think logically.

Self-sufficiency never really worked for me—a fact which the magnitude of caring for my mother's needs forced me to admit. The problem was that I viewed God's favor (or possible lack thereof) on my life through the lens of a pre-Christian past, so I listened to my feelings when they told me that God had been absent during the painful times of my childhood when I most needed Him. I had not known my heavenly Father's faithful character, or how to speak the faith-language of His kingdom. Thus, I had serious doubts about whether I could actually cast all of my cares upon His shoulders. Little did I realize that He was only a moment away at any given time! I now understand that God did not cause the difficulties I faced in dealing with my parents; however, He did use those painful wilderness experiences to steer me in the direction of the cross.

We live in a fallen world. Pain and difficulty are inevitable. Anyone who says differently is conveniently ignoring the full message of Christ. Still, from before the foundation of the world, our loving, faithful God prepared the answer to our every need. He looks after the details—even the small ones—in ways beyond our comprehension. Yes, we will face times of extreme difficulty as we journey through this life, but He always provides the abundant grace needed to handle the challenges of each and every day. It is only when we attempt to carry *The Weight of Tomorrow* that we lose the strength to effectively live for Christ today.

The Lord did indeed provide a sacrificial ram for Abraham on that fateful day. Many years later, He provided the Lamb of God as a sacrifice for all sin so that we each might have the opportunity to become God's covenant children. If our Father loved us enough to go to such extremes, we can be sure that every other need along the way will be met in its time.

PROBING QUESTIONS

Why do we so often attempt to carry tomorrow's burdens upon today's shoulders?

What cumulative effect does this have?

How can trauma from our past adversely influence our ability to trust God today?

ACTION STEP

Write out a list of future concerns that might be weighing you down. Repent of your unbelief and prayerfully surrender them to God, believing that He cares more about the need than you do.

CLOSING PRAYER

Father, please forgive me for carrying burdens that I was never designed to carry. I surrender each and every need to You, believing that You will supply all of my needs.

FURTHER READING

Matthew 6:25-34; John 16:25-33; Romans 8:31-39

CHAPTER THIRTY-FOUR
ENEMIES IN THE WILDERNESS

There are two equal and opposite errors into which our race can fall about the devils. One is to disbelieve in their existence. The other is to believe, and to feel an excessive and unhealthy interest in them. They themselves are equally pleased by both errors and hail a materialist or a magician with the same delight.

–C.S. Lewis, scholar and author

"Remember what the Amalekites did to you on the journey after you left Egypt. They met you along the way and attacked all your stragglers from behind when you were tired and weary. They did not fear God."
DEUTERONOMY 25:17-18 (HCSB)

Years ago, I felt led by the Holy Spirit to reach out to what I like to call a "counter-cultural" group at our local university. Their loosely structured goal was to promote a radical leftist agenda in an attempt to make our world a better place. Many of these students were "black", not black as in African American, but black as in *goth*; often sporting tattoos, boldly colored hair, and multiple piercings. I was in my thirties, probably bearing a closer resemblance to a redneck than a college graduate. It goes without saying that I did not fit in well.

My efforts to reach out were complicated by a weekly pattern that I can only describe as spiritual warfare. Beginning anywhere from three to five o'clock in the afternoon, I would begin to feel a pit in my stomach—even if I was not consciously thinking about the upcoming meeting. By the time the nine o'clock meeting drew near, I felt absolutely miserable, wishing I could crawl into bed and curl up into the fetal position for the remainder of the evening. Each week, however, I would drag myself to the car and head toward campus. Whether it was out of simple obedience, or my own stubbornness, I don't really know.

While at the meetings, I would be bombarded by negative thoughts. "What are you doing here? Why are you wasting your time? You don't belong! You'll never be able to impact these people!" Again, I would press through the difficulties, sometimes managing an awkward conversation or two with the students or their sponsoring professor.

After the meeting, things always took an interesting turn as I drove the few short blocks toward home. The sense of oppression would quickly lift and suddenly the world seemed like a much better and more welcoming place. Once again God would feel near and faith no longer seemed unattainable. This entire transition would take place within about a five-minute time span.

I'm no rocket scientist, but it did not take long for me to realize that I was dealing with some type of spiritual oppression. Since that time, I have seen a multitude of these demonic attacks, not only against me, but directed at all who are involved with front-line ministry. C.S. Lewis knew what he was talking about. To focus on Satan and other demonic spirits is downright dangerous, but to completely ignore them is nothing short of foolish. Winning a war is next to impossible when one's enemies are not clearly defined.

The powers of darkness will use whatever means possible to bring people down. In what some call "primitive" cultures, they tend to rule by force and intimidation, controlling people through the power of fear. In more "civilized" environments, deceptive stealth becomes the primary tactic; those demons will weave a web of deception that conceals their very existence.

I find it sad and ironic that many of us are so adversely affected by Satan's deceitful schemes. Possessing no real power over the people of God, he instead employs clever tactics and mind games to compel us to destroy ourselves—and one another. Victory, however, is ours if only we will reach out and lay hold of it. Our ability to recognize and disarm demonic tactics means a great deal when it comes to healthy spiritual living and effective ministry.

God is not the author of all wilderness experiences. Yes, He frequently calls us away from the crowds to spend one-on-one time with Him, but those aren't intended to be periods of loneliness and isolation. Other people may give us grief, but no one created in the image of God is truly a foe. Understanding such things is critical because, just as the Amalekites attacked the vulnerable Israelite stragglers, Satan habitually uses the wilderness to separate and destroy the people of God.

The natural world provides us with some clear illustrations of this principle. How does the lion kill the wildebeest? Isolation! African wildebeest are dangerous in a herd, working closely together for safety and strength. Rather than risk personal injury, lions will painstakingly separate a lone individual from the safety of its herd. Most of us have seen the documentaries in which an unfortunate creature is pulled to the ground and ravenously devoured.

Isn't it interesting that when we are struggling, our natural tendency is to run from God and to isolate ourselves from His people? Our hearts fill with a sense of inadequacy, often resulting in bitter judgments toward those who genuinely care about us. The last thing we want is for other people to catch even a glimpse of our struggles, making us especially vulnerable to deceptive tactics. Do we really think that such feelings and thoughts are without demonic influence?

Always, always, always, we must learn to run *to* God and never away, regardless of how many times we fail or how intense our struggles feel. Just as Jesus utilized the Scriptures during His forty-day fast to defeat the devil's tactics, so we too must learn to rightly understand and employ the word of God. Also vital are deliberate and persistent efforts to emotionally connect with others whenever possible. Mutual support, encouragement, and even correction have always been integral to God's plan for the well-being of His people.

Don't marvel that fallen angels (demons) are so angry and cruel. They are frustrated and fearful, fully aware of the impending doom that constantly looms over their heads (Matthew 8:29). In the wilderness, we will never fail to encounter these "wild beasts" who seek to rob and destroy all that is good. Still, there is no balance of power between good and evil. By pursuing truth, abiding in grace, and connecting with God's people we can—and will—defeat their every dark scheme!

PROBING QUESTIONS

Why do so many of our spiritual battles take place in our minds?

Why is it foolish for us to run from God when we are struggling?

Why is it a huge mistake to think that people are our enemies?

ACTION STEP

If you are struggling with any type of personal issue, immediately take it to your heavenly Father in prayer and with complete honesty. You may also want to pick up the phone and call or message someone.

CLOSING PRAYER

Jesus, I thank You so much that You are my faithful High Priest who understands my every struggle. Help me learn to always run quickly and directly to You whenever I am struggling.

FURTHER READING

Matthew 4:1-11; Ephesians 6:10-18; Hebrews 3:12-14, 4:14-16

CHAPTER THIRTY-FIVE
IF GOD IS FOR US, WHY IS SO MUCH AGAINST US?

Adversity is the diamond dust heaven polishes its jewels with.
–Robert Leighton, pastor and scholar

When David and his men arrived at the town, they found it burned down. Their wives, sons, and daughters had been kidnapped. David and the troops with him wept loudly until they had no strength left to weep. David's two wives, Ahinoam the Jezreelite and Abigail the widow of Nabal the Carmelite, had also been kidnapped. David was in a difficult position because the troops talked about stoning him, for they were all very bitter over the loss of their sons and daughters. But David found strength in the LORD his God.

1 SAMUEL 30:3-6 (HCSB)

One of the greatest athletes of our time is Michael Phelps—winner of twenty-two Olympic medals. Once, while watching Phelps perform, I found myself intrigued as the announcers spoke of his relationship with longtime coach, Bob Bowman. Bowman, it seems, had a habit of purposefully making Michael's life difficult. In one instance, he intentionally stepped on the swimmer's goggles just prior to a race; Phelps was forced to swim virtually blind as the lenses filled with pool water. Interestingly, Michael's goggles did accidentally fill with water in the 200-meter butterfly during the 2008 Beijing Olympics.

Phelps still won gold. Coach Bowman had wisely prepared his young champion for virtually anything he would face in the pool.

As the greatest coach ever, God's discipline in the lives of His children is always formative and never punitive. His goal is to shape us into champions, and He is quite efficient at using whatever means available to accomplish that task. This does not mean, however, that we should passively embrace all forms of adversity as coming from the hand of God. David didn't strengthen himself in the Lord because it seemed like the spiritual thing to do. He sought God's guidance and strength so that he could rescue his family.

David knew he had adversaries—even some from his own ranks—but he never saw his God as a part of the problem. Instead of miring himself in a mud pit of despair and complaint, David would begin crying out to God about his problems and end by worshipping his faithful Lord. (Psalm 22 is a possible product of this particular wilderness experience.) The end result was not bitterness but newfound strength in the Lord. As an expression of his faith, David would then seek God's wisdom and guidance for the next steps to be taken. An overwhelming victory over his enemies always followed.

One might wonder why David, who was highly favored by the God of heaven, had to go through such difficulty. To put it in more familiar terms, I sometimes have people ask, as they face adversity on multiple fronts, if I think God or Satan is at work. My answer is usually, "Yes," and no, I am not being elusive. We live in a fallen, decaying world. We have very real enemies. Difficult times are inevitable, but thankfully our God is the ultimate "spin-master" when it comes to turning every adverse circumstance to our benefit.

The truth is that multiple things can be happening at once. This world has enough trouble in and of itself. The devil's lackeys can be attacking us as we experience the fallout of a broken world, we can unwittingly bring difficulties upon ourselves, and God can be using the entire process to train us into champions. In David's case, the heavenly Father's mysterious hand used every difficult circumstance to prepare a king for the throne of His beloved nation. I can't help but wonder how many others (like King Saul, for example) God sought to prepare, but who failed to align themselves with God's design.

My spouse works for a building contractor, so visiting the tire shop is a common occurrence for me; she tends to pick up stray nails and screws from driving in that environment. There, sitting on the counter of Lias Tire, is a large jar full of objects of every sort that have been removed from people's tires. Issues are always going to arise in that place where the rubber meets the road. Those of us who are God's covenant children live on the horizon where heaven meets earth. How can we expect things to always go our way when we dwell where the kingdoms of light and darkness collide?

I once read a book in which the author spoke of Christ's obscure childhood, commenting that Satan was probably unaware of the Son of God living in Nazareth. I chuckled. I can promise you that if a person lives even one month without sinning, he or she will have all of hell's attention. Jesus Himself said that His followers can expect persecution of various sorts (John 15:18-21, 16:1-4, 17:14-18). Those are the types of "promises" we prefer not to confess.

There are days, sometimes even extended seasons, when we wonder where God has gotten Himself off to. With so many difficulties facing us, it can feel as though He has taken a long vacation without bothering to inform us of His absence. Seeking God's wisdom is essential in adverse circumstances because there is no predetermined formula for overcoming. Sometimes we need to passively surrender control to our Lord. Another appropriate approach is to praise and worship our way through our struggles. Still, in other situations, we must stand up and fight for all that is true.

Through the very same circumstances which Satan seeks to break us, God will establish us. How we respond to such adversity is what makes the difference. But regardless of how we should handle any given circumstance, one thing will always ring true: no matter how things look at any given moment, our God is for us and never against us. He is never malicious, or absent, or even forgetful. Our Lord and Savior is always at work, in one way or another, on our behalf. We must be convinced of this reality if we are to reign victorious through our faithful God.

PROBING QUESTIONS
Why is discipline a sign of love?

What does it mean to say that God's discipline for His children is formative and not punitive?

Why is it essential to seek God's wisdom in the midst of adverse circumstances?

ACTION STEP
Look back over your life and recount a time when you thought God was against you, only to later realize that He was actually working in your favor.

CLOSING PRAYER
Father, as the source and giver of all wisdom, I ask You to open my eyes and grant me discernment as I seek to overcome the challenges I face.

FURTHER READING
1 Samuel 30; Romans 5:1-5; Hebrews 12:4-13; James 1:1-8

CHAPTER THIRTY-SIX
AROUND THE MOUNTAIN

The success or failure of our work as a church or mission depends, in the last resort, largely, not in the number of preachers we put into the field, nor on the size of our congregations, but rather on the character of Christianity we and our work produce.
— Duncan Campbell, preacher and revivalist

"Then we turned and set out for the wilderness by the way to the Red Sea, as the LORD spoke to me, and circled Mount Seir for many days. And the LORD spoke to me, saying, 'You have circled this mountain long enough.'"
DEUTERONOMY 2:1-3A (NASB)

Few things are more frustrating—or scary—than hiking through a wilderness only to find oneself unintentionally returning to the same place. I remember an occasion when I was hunting in semi-familiar territory near the top of a hill. Deceived by the contour of the ridge, I thought I was heading in the direction of my SUV when, in fact, I looped back to the same place where I had stood less than an hour prior. Tempted to panic, I took some time to re-examine the landscape, setting out once again in the same direction. This time I saw my error and made it to my vehicle without further incident.

There is no escaping the God-ordained reality that genuine progress in life is dependent upon character growth. Through the general course of our lives, God is more concerned about what is going on inside of us than He is with where we are going. That's not to say that direction in life is unimportant, only that it is secondary to character development. The person formed into the image of Christ can be used by God anywhere across the face of this earth. The one with flawed character will inevitably wreak havoc in those very same places.

It is not beyond our Lord to use adverse circumstances for disciplinary purposes as He transforms us into the image of Christ. As a loving Father, His desire is always to form and never to punish. All too often, however, we conveniently ignore what He is trying to accomplish, usually blaming all unfavorable circumstances on the actions of others.

How can we tell when the Great Sculptor of the Universe is trying to shape our character? We tune our ear to His, taking deliberate care to look for patterns. If you find yourself saying, "Why does this always happen to me?" there is a good chance that some type of character issue is at play. During such times, I often pray for wisdom, asking my Father what it is that He wants to accomplish in my life.

Does it matter whether or not we know what God is after? In some situations it absolutely does! If we know what He is doing, we can get on board with the process, often shortening the duration and intensity of the trial. But if we remain oblivious to His plans and purposes, we will face similar circumstances somewhere down the road. You can be sure of one thing: the obstacles will be bigger and more intimidating the next time around. Eventually, we will come to a place where the barriers are so large that we have no choice but to deal with our issues.

Much can be learned through study and prayer, but true growth must be tested through the fires of adversity. Unfortunately for us, this usually involves pain of one type or another, but it is wise to distinguish between "good" pain and "bad" pain. Good pain serves to further mold and shape our character. Bad pain amounts to eating the unpleasant fruit of our own foolish choices. We can learn and grow from bad pain, but a little personal honesty seasoned with courage will help us avoid its bitter taste.

I remember a time when I felt abandoned by a friend. I had invested a considerable amount of time and energy into our relationship with the hopes of accomplishing great things for God together. Having experienced a pattern of abandonment in the past, this situation released a torrent of latent pain that quickly overwhelmed me. In an effort to cope, I trudged out to work in my garden, licking my wounds and lamenting the raw deal I had been dealt. Much to my dismay, the Holy Spirit spoke some surprising words to my heart. "You asked for this, you know." "Yeah right," was my response. He continued with, "You asked to be conformed into the image of Jesus. He was abandoned by others and I am giving you the opportunity to be made more like Him."

What a relief it was to hear that my God had not abandoned me! Nor were my circumstances a form of punishment. Suddenly, my pain wasn't all that bad. My heavenly Father was working through my circumstances, answering my prayers in powerful, albeit mysterious ways. His goal is always to form us, never to belittle or destroy.

Are there any among us who don't dream of becoming champions in life? Our victory is our Father's passion! Like a wise and caring coach, He molds and shapes us to fulfill dreams we never even knew we had. This leaves us each with the ongoing choice of joining His heavenly game plan in preparation for future exploits, or sulking and complaining about our difficulties.

Would you rather grow in God's grace, or take yet another proverbial trip *Around the Mountain*? If you can be honest with yourself, if you can pray for wisdom (and really mean it), if you can recognize disciplinary patterns in your life, then you can become a willing participant in the champion-growing process. How much better for us to get with God's program than to spend our days in bewilderment, complaining about the same problems time and time again!

PROBING QUESTIONS

Why is personal honesty so important when dealing with life's challenges?

Are you more concerned about the strength of your character, or about where you go and what you do?

Why must true character growth always be tested?

ACTION STEP
Think back over the past two or three months of your life. Have you found yourself saying, "Why does this always happen to me?" Take some time to seek God's wisdom in an effort to discover what He might be trying to accomplish in you.

CLOSING PRAYER
Heavenly Father, thank You so much that You don't use us and then discard us, but that You always seek to grow us into the image of Jesus. Please grant me the wisdom to recognize Your loving hand at work in my life.

FURTHER READING
1 Corinthians 10:1-13; Romans 8:28-29; Hebrews 12:1-11

CHAPTER THIRTY-SEVEN
OUR COVENANT KING

*There is no more blessed way of living than the life of faith upon
a covenant-keeping God—to know that we have no care, for he
careth for us, that we need have no fear, except to fear him, that
we need have no troubles, because we have cast our burdens upon
the Lord, and are conscious that he will sustain us.*

–Charles Spurgeon, pastor and author

**Then all the congregation of the sons of Israel journeyed
by stages from the wilderness of Sin, according to the
command of the LORD, and camped at Rephidim, and
there was no water for the people to drink. Therefore the
people quarreled with Moses and said, "Give us water
that we may drink." And Moses said to them, "Why do you
quarrel with me? Why do you test the LORD?" But the people
thirsted there for water; and they grumbled against Moses
and said, "Why, now, have you brought us up from Egypt,
to kill us and our children and our livestock with thirst?" . . .
He named the place Massah and Meribah because of the
quarrel of the sons of Israel, and because they tested the
LORD, saying, "Is the LORD among us, or not?"**

EXODUS 17:1-3, 7 (NASB)

As a child, I once watched a movie in which an old man encouraged
his grandson to do wrong things and then acted like it was entirely
the boy's choosing, essentially hanging him out to dry when the
poor kid got in trouble for his misguided actions. For reasons that

I can't explain, I somehow felt that this terrible pattern was also characteristic of God, that He leads people into courses of action that cause them considerable suffering, only to enjoy watching silently from a distance as they squirm. It is impossible for me to say this more emphatically: like the Israelites' twisted perspective at Meribah, my childhood lens was grossly distorted!

When Adam and Eve ate from the tree of the knowledge of good and evil, they chose to distance themselves from God, seeking instead a path of independence. How quickly those unfortunate souls must have realized the unbearable burden that they had pulled squarely upon their own shoulders! Attempting to be like God apart from God makes humans debtors to perfection; it is a debt that we can never possibly pay.

The Bible records that Adam and Eve withdrew into the shadows, hiding in shame as the contrast between their sin-stained selves and the perfectly magnificent Creator became all too clear. Born was the fear that total disclosure is the precursor of abandonment, an inherent belief that rejection is inevitable as soon as others see the "real" me. The only practical solution, it seemed, was to hide from His penetrating gaze. I don't think their approach worked out all that well.

Since that fateful day in the garden, the fear of abandonment has been ingrained in the human psyche. And because a covenant worldview is now found only in movie fantasies, the problem of abandonment has increased in both scope and intensity. Today, we have husbands deserting their wives for younger women, mothers leaving their children to do drugs, companies jilting their employees due to greed, and governments forsaking their citizens for the sake of political gain. Add an almost endless list of other forms of abandonment common to our culture, and it should be no surprise that we often find ourselves feeling insecure and anxious.

To our detriment, our view of God can be tainted by the shortcomings of unfaithful humans. All too often, our lack of confidence in others morphs into a lack of trust in God and His promises. Like a shark patiently cruising under the surface of the ocean in search of its prey, our underlying uncertainties linger beneath the surface of our hearts, surging quickly to tear at our souls when we enter unfamiliar and adverse wilderness territory.

If we take but a minute to stop and reflect, we will come to realize that a lack of trust in God makes absolutely no sense for a Christian. Our King is all-powerful and full of love, ever faithful to His word, fulfilling each and every promise He makes along the way. If we truly believed in the goodness of God toward His children, we would never—even for a moment—doubt that He will be there to meet our every need. And yet, doubt we do—a lot! Fear and doubt, inherent to our fallen natures, deceive us with feelings that scream loudly: "God has forgotten me!" We are blind, totally misunderstanding the true nature and character of our loving Lord.

Foreseeing our fear, worry, and anxiety, our Father provided the opportunity for us to envision His absolute faithfulness by instituting, the concept of a *blood covenant—a sacred and binding relationship*, similar to a blood brotherhood as might be seen in a movie. Intended to be unbreakable in nature, it amounts to what we might call a *super-glued* relationship. The first covenants were established in the garden of Eden, and since that time, God's interaction with His beloved children has taken place through a series of covenants.

The New Covenant is a blood covenant, established by Jesus with the price that He willingly paid for our sins (see 1 Corinthians 11:25). All of this points us toward our absolutely faithful Father; we can trust Him with total confidence regardless of how horrible our circumstances may appear. There may be times when we don't understand God's actions (or inaction), but we can always trust His faithful love.

The beauty of the gospel is that we don't need to be perfect for God to fulfill His promises to us. In a very real sense, God's faithfulness has nothing to do with our worthiness (or lack thereof), and everything to do with the nature of His character. If our loving Lord leads us somewhere, we can be sure that it is with a good purpose and that He will never abandon us in the process. Whether the winds of our lives are favorable or fierce, let us be sure to place the full weight of our trust in our *Covenant King*!

PROBING QUESTIONS

Why do our imperfections cause us to fear that others will abandon us?

What is it about unknown wilderness territory that brings our fears to the surface?

In what ways is a blood covenant intended to provide a tangible illustration of our heavenly Father's faithful love?

ACTION STEP

List all of the examples of covenants that you can and identify the common threads between them.

CLOSING PRAYER

Heavenly Father, please open my eyes to Your undying love. Help me to respond in kind.

FURTHER READING

Genesis 3:1-10; Joshua 1:1-9; Psalms 89:1-18, 34-37

CHAPTER THIRTY-EIGHT
BUT GOD REMEMBERED NOAH ...

*So many times we say that we can't serve God because we aren't
whatever is needed. We're not talented enough or smart enough
or whatever. But if you are in covenant with Jesus Christ, He is
responsible for covering your weaknesses, for being your strength.
He will give you His abilities for your disabilities!*
–Kay Arthur, Bible teacher and author

But God remembered Noah ...

GENESIS 8:1 (NASB)

So many years of hard labor to build the ark—was it really God's
leading, or merely the bizarre vision of a crazy man? The tension
would have been thick in Noah's household as the entire family
wrestled with the realization that loved ones would be lost in the
deluge. And then, Noah had only seven days to gather all of the
animals and load them onto the ark—all of the work, the chaos, the
destruction, the emotional exhaustion!

Forty days and forty nights of constant, heavy rain would dwarf
any of our worst camping experiences. In the midst of seemingly
endless days, dwelling in the sunless hull of a manure-filled boat
aimlessly adrift on a lonely sea, more than once Noah might have
seriously doubted whether he would ever see the birth of a new
and better world. If Noah didn't have such faith struggles, he was
probably hounded by family members who did.

But God remembered Noah . . . Why did God remember? In
part, because Noah was a righteous man—his heart was not inclined

toward evil as was the rest of the human race. We also know that Noah understood the importance of a blood sacrifice in atoning for sins (Genesis 8:20), because without the shedding of blood there is no forgiveness of sins (Hebrews 9:22). The stain of our sins must be fully addressed if we are to somehow relate to a pure and holy Creator. Noah had found favor, and so God made a covenant through which He proved Himself faithful to meet the man's every need.

As Noah's adventure came to an end, God reaffirmed the blessing of fruitfulness first given in the garden of Eden, and then promised never to flood the entire earth again. In the process, He established the rainbow as a sign of this unconditional promise (Genesis 9:1-17). Heaven has before it constant reminders of God's covenant relationship with the Earth and all of its inhabitants (Ezekiel 1:27-28; Revelation 4:3, 10:1). Not that they are needed—faithfulness is at the very core of God's nature. We are the ones who need to be reminded because we are so apt to drift into doubt, fear, and anxiety.

Interestingly, the Hebrew language does not have its own unique word for "rainbow". Instead the term "war-bow" is used.

> *The meaning seems to be that what was ordinarily an instrument of war, and a symbol of vengeance, became a symbol of peace and mercy by virtue of its now being set in the clouds. Against the black storm clouds God's war-bow is transformed into a rainbow by the sunlight of his mercy and grace. God is at peace with his covenant people.*[4]

Noah's covenant story of salvation provides invaluable insight for those of us who are children of God through faith in Christ. Peter wrote that Noah's experience is a picture (type) of water baptism into Christ (1 Peter 3:18-22). Through faith in His atoning sacrifice on the cross, we are washed of wicked stains, previously indelible due to our sins. Clothing ourselves in Christ's "robe of righteousness" (Isaiah 61:10), we receive amazing—though undeserved—favor with the Creator of the Universe, Through baptism, we surrender control of our lives to our Lord and Savior, trusting Him to raise us up into a new and higher life. This is the essence of the blood covenant commonly known as the New Covenant.

On a personal level, understanding the nature of our covenant relationship with God has been instrumental in helping me to abide in His peace throughout the rigors of my own faith journey. I am no stranger to inner turmoil. Through much of my life, I have battled against a sense of inadequacy from within and a host of adversities from without. One spring day, many years ago, I was fishing at a local lake, but my mind was lost in struggle. I felt beyond hope; the dark storm clouds overhead served as an appropriate metaphor for my inner anguish. Suddenly, a double rainbow formed in the distance, its brilliance accentuated by the dark storm clouds in the background. What a reminder that, even in my extreme weakness, I was still His child!

About twenty years later, Debi and I began our new ministry with very little money and only a small base of support. Soon after, we were graciously given a well-built house next to the Indiana University of Pennsylvania (IUP) campus to use as a ministry center. The problem was that we didn't have any money to make renovations and bring the building up to code. Still, we pressed forward as the finances trickled in.

One afternoon, a rainstorm passed through as I raked gravel to complete the new parking area. Our renter, Sharon, approached me with an envelope she had just pulled from the mailbox. A beautiful rainbow spread across the sky just as I pulled out fifty dollars in cash. Through that anonymous gift, my heavenly Father reminded me that He was still my Covenant Provider! He continued to meet every need as we completed that entire renovation project without borrowing a penny. Just as God had remembered Noah, so too, He remembered us.

In addition to learning to stand on the promises of God, three things have helped to remind me of God's faithfulness to His covenants. The rainbow is one. My water baptism experience is another. Serving as my "initiation ceremony" into the New Covenant, I can always recall that experience during those times when I doubt the nature of my relationship with Christ the Savior. (If you haven't been water baptized, please see Appendix II.) Finally, to help settle my ever wandering heart, taking communion serves as an intentional, ongoing reminder of Christ's absolute devotion. Heaven needs no reminders of the covenant between God and His children, but if we are to abide in His peace, we most certainly do.

PROBING QUESTIONS
Why did God remember Noah?

What role does water baptism play in the New Covenant?

How can a clearer understanding of our covenant relationship with God help us to be at peace through difficult times?

ACTION STEP
Tell someone today about your personal water baptism experience. If you haven't been water baptized, please read Appendix II to evaluate the nature of your relationship with God.

CLOSING PRAYER
Heavenly Father, I thank You for Your immeasurable faithfulness to Your children. Help me to better understand Your nature, and to be faithful to You and Your people in return.

FURTHER READING
Genesis 6, 7, 8, 9:1-17

CHAPTER THIRTY-NINE
WHEN GOD CHANGED HIS NAME

Our faith was also prefigured in Abraham. . . . Know ye therefore, that they which are of faith, the same are the children of Abraham. [Abraham's] faith and ours are one and the same.
–Irenaeus, second-century church father

Then Moses said to God, "Behold, I am going to the sons of Israel, and I will say to them, 'The God of your fathers has sent me to you.' Now they may say to me, 'What is His name?' What shall I say to them?" God said to Moses, "I AM WHO I AM"; and He said, "Thus you shall say to the sons of Israel, 'I AM has sent me to you.'" God, furthermore, said to Moses, "Thus you shall say to the sons of Israel, 'The LORD [YHWH or Yahweh], the God of your fathers, the God of Abraham, the God of Isaac, and the God of Jacob, has sent me to you.' This is My name forever, and this is My memorial-name to all generations."

EXODUS 3:13-15 (NASB)

For God to describe Himself as "I AM WHO I AM" makes perfect sense to me, even if I don't comprehend the full ramifications of such a statement. God always was. God is. God always will be. God is always present. The Creator of all things is the very essence of being, as well He should be. It is from God that all of creation flows; He needs or relies upon nothing for the sake of His existence. God is who He is regardless of who we are, or what we do.

And yet, the eternal God identified Himself to Moses as, "The LORD, the God of your fathers, the God of Abraham, the God of Isaac, and the God of Jacob." This was to be His "memorial-name to all generations"—that is the name by which all Israelites throughout the ages were to remember their God. I understand that down through history most of the emphasis from this passage has been placed upon "Yahweh" (translated as "LORD") as the primary name that God was communicating. In the context of the Old Testament, this view appears to be entirely appropriate. Still, I can't help but think that the ancient Israelites missed an integral aspect of what God was communicating to Moses.

The ancient Jewish perspective saw God as *transcendent*—being so *far removed from sinful humans* (and so revered) that the name Yahweh was never spoken. But from the context of this passage, we see that God chose to link His self-existence to His covenant relationship with Abraham, Isaac, Jacob, and their descendants. This wasn't just the name of a distant, self-existing God, but of one who chose to identify Himself by His connection with sinful humans. Jesus, God in human form, further addressed this issue by introducing the LORD as our heavenly *Father*—a covenantal title. Such is the nature of covenant as even identities become shared.

The Apostle Paul went on to teach that all who embrace the New Covenant in Christ become the spiritual descendants of Abraham (Galatians 3:6-9). In other words, the memorial-name, "The LORD, the God of your fathers, the God of Abraham, the God of Isaac, and the God of Jacob," applies not only to the physical descendants of Abraham, but to all who are truly Christian. We are included in the generations referred to in Exodus 3:15, as evidenced by the "spirit of adoption as sons by which we cry out, 'Abba, Father!'" (Romans 8:15).

When I consider the immensity of our eternal God, that He created the Universe with billions of galaxies containing billions of stars in each, my brain begins to overheat. Further still, the very thought that our all-powerful Creator would choose to identify Himself by His relationship with humans stretches the boundaries of my comprehension. This speaks not of distance and supremacy, but of love and intimacy, of an ever faithful friendship.

What will you do when you get beyond the confines of what you consider to be civilization? How will you react when you find yourself beyond necessary comforts, beyond visible provision, beyond the use of a cell phone? How will you respond in the midst of a spiritual wasteland where God appears to have abandoned you?

Job refused to curse God. Abraham believed God. Moses walked in humble obedience. Daniel and his friends spurned every temptation to compromise the integrity of their faith. David turned his complaints into praise. Paul refused to yield to despair. These men were all champions of the faith—and of the same spiritual DNA from which we are formed.

God gave Himself a "memorial-name" so that those under the Mosaic Law would remember the covenant relationship He had established with their forefathers. Today, we celebrate the memorial that we call "communion" as a tangible reminder of God's ever present faithfulness. Each time we come together to share in the bread and the wine (or juice) we are renewing our remembrance of our blood covenant with the heavenly Father through Jesus Christ.

Again, it isn't God who needs to be reminded of these things— such loving faithfulness is integral to His very nature. We, however, must call them to mind because we are prone to lose sight of His faithfulness. We have no choice but to remember if we are to emerge triumphant over the darkness of this world. As we journey through shadow-filled valleys and arid wastelands, we would be foolish not to lay hold of the extreme level of devotion our heavenly Father feels toward His children. Only from such a rock-solid sense of covenantal identity can faith freely flow.

How the deepest parts of my soul are stirred when I think that the King of kings and Lord of lords willingly chooses to identify Himself by His relationship with us, His children! As the great "I AM," He is self-existent and able to do anything He pleases. But as the God of our Fathers, the God of Abraham, the God of Isaac, and the God of Jacob, we know that we are always on His mind and in His heart. As the Creator of the Universe, He has every right to be distant from broken humanity, but as our heavenly *Abba* (an intimate term similar to *Daddy*), He instead chooses to draw us securely into His ever faithful arms.

PROBING QUESTIONS

What thoughts come to mind when you consider the idea that God chooses to identify Himself through His relationship with humans?

What does this say about where we should find our primary source of identity?

How can memorial practices such as communion serve to strengthen us through wilderness seasons?

ACTION STEP

Pray the Lord's Prayer (Matthew 6:9-13) out loud substituting "My Father" for "Our Father."

CLOSING PRAYER

God of Abraham, Isaac, and Jacob, help me to know in my heart of hearts that You are my loving Father, and that I can find my security in Your ever faithful arms.

FURTHER READING

Genesis 15:1-6, Psalms 23; Matthew 6:5-15; 1 Corinthians 11:23-26

STAGE FOUR
JOURNEYING WITH A PURPOSE

I am prepared to go anywhere, provided it be forward. I determined never to stop until I had come to the end and achieved my purpose.

—David Livingstone, missionary and explorer

"This is My commandment, that you love one another, just as I have loved you. Greater love has no one than this, that one lay down his life for his friends. You are My friends if you do what I command you. No longer do I call you slaves, for the slave does not know what his master is doing; but I have called you friends, for all things that I have heard from My Father I have made known to you. You did not choose Me but I chose you, and appointed you that you would go and bear fruit, and that your fruit would remain, so that whatever you ask of the Father in My name He may give to you."
JOHN 15:12-16 (NASB)

Quite often, we consider wilderness experiences to be dark and meaningless, but those who use such opportunities to grasp hold of their Savior will one day emerge with a profound sense of purpose. As we finish Stage Four, the last leg of our journey together, we'll come to understand that our loving Father fully intends to use even our worst experiences not only to establish us, but also to help others.

CHAPTER FORTY
REDEFINING WHO YOU ARE

The major strategy of Satan is to distort the character of God and the truth of who we are. He can't change God and he can't do anything to change our identity and position in Christ. If, however, he can get us to believe a lie, we will live as though our identity in Christ isn't true.

–Neil T. Anderson, scholar and author

As soon as he had finished speaking to Saul, the soul of Jonathan was knit to the soul of David, and Jonathan loved him as his own soul. And Saul took him that day and would not let him return to his father's house. Then Jonathan made a covenant with David, because he loved him as his own soul. And Jonathan stripped himself of the robe that was on him and gave it to David, and his armor, and even his sword and his bow and his belt.

1 SAMUEL 18:1-4 (ESV)

As a kid, I watched my share of cowboy movies on television. The hero was usually a strong, masculine, self-sufficient character who rode off alone into the sunset at the end of the story. The common folk merely stood by and watched in awe as this larger than life figure faded into the distant horizon. The solitary cowboy's glory fed every little boy's dreams.

Rugged individualism may have its benefits, but there are not many. The individualistic mindset of the West has contributed to the decay of the nuclear family—a breakdown which spells certain destruction for any culture. At its core, the glory of individualism is nothing more than a deadly and destructive myth. From the very beginning of time as we know it, God determined that "it is not good for man to be alone" (Genesis 2:18). None of us came into this world by our own effort and none of us can prosper apart from the investment of others.

If individualism is so unhealthy, why do we value it to the degree that we do? In part, we can look to those movies that I watched as a child; their romantic images found a home in many a young boy's heart. But such unrealistic visions don't stay around unless they somehow resonate with our natural drives and tendencies. (For example, I've watched a few "chick flicks" in my day but none have been added to my personal movie collection.)

At the roots of individualism, men especially find a mistaken sense of identity, somehow thinking that strength, toughness, and performance define who we are. From a covenant perspective, however, we are not defined by what we do, but rather by who we are in relationship to others—especially to our Creator.

Jonathan's robe and armor were unique identifiers of the rightful heir to the throne of Israel. Giving them to David redefined, at least to a degree, David's identity. When other Israelites saw David wearing Jonathan's robe, they knew immediately that any disrespect would bring the wrath of the prince of Israel upon their heads. A sharing of identities exemplifies the very heart of a God-ordained covenant.

God seems to have no problem redefining the identities of His covenant children. He did it with Abraham (previously Abram), the father of our faith, and He did it with Peter (previously Simon), one of the more eminent apostles. The truth, however, is that regardless of whether or not there is a formal name change, God reconstructs the identity of every one of His children. Upon entry into the Christian faith, every person's identity is redefined as a son or daughter of the King of kings and Lord of lords. The full ramifications of this new sense of significance push the limits of human comprehension.

Indeed, one of most problematic issues in the church today is that we don't know who we are as the covenant children of God. Such insecurity leads to a host of problems. Seeing ourselves as miserable worms and beggars in the eyes of the holy God, we muddle along with hearts full of fear and anxiety, hoping that for some vague reason He will look upon us with momentary favor.

True confidence grows from the inside out, not the outside in. We are validated not by our performance and the subsequent approval of others, but by the reality of our covenant relationship with God. It is no trite matter to be called a child of God and to be clothed in Christ's robe of righteousness.

The line between confidence in God and arrogance may at times appear to be very fine, but it is a line nonetheless. In reality, a true understanding of our covenant identity in God will free us from pride and arrogance. When we know who we are, we have no need to climb the ladder of significance, or broadcast our strengths to others. When we know who we are, we are free to just be, to walk with God, and to serve Him (and others) without constantly focusing on our own self-worth, or lack thereof.

We too often get bogged down in the wilderness because of a vain effort to find significance within ourselves apart from God. This inherent, yet painfully destructive, tendency must be thoroughly addressed if we are to live with a healthy sense of purpose. Thus, our loving Father will deconstruct our old, flesh-based identities in order to establish the new. If you feel like God is tearing you down, it is only for the purpose of building you up. Never allow doubt to take root in your heart during such times. Instead, lay hold of your covenant identity in Christ, and in due season you will find yourself overflowing with life.

PROBING QUESTIONS

What are some ways in which individualism is detrimental?

Why are we so tempted to establish our sense of identity by what we do?

What can we do to lay hold of an eternal and unshakeable identity through our relationship with the heavenly Father?

ACTION STEP

List some of the areas of life in which you have tried to find a sense of significance. Compare how much work is involved in these efforts with what it takes to be called a child of God.

CLOSING PRAYER

Heavenly Father, please open my eyes to the reality of my unshakeable identity in You through the New Covenant in Jesus Christ.

FURTHER READING

John 1:1-13; 2 Corinthians 5:16-21; Philippians 3:1-7; 1 Peter 2:4-10

CHAPTER FORTY-ONE
A POWERFUL CURE FOR APATHY

Science may have found a cure for most evils; but it has found no remedy for the worst of them all—the apathy of human beings.
—Helen Keller, political activist and author

One day the angel of GOD came and sat down under the oak in Ophrah that belonged to Joash the Abiezrite, whose son Gideon was threshing wheat in the winepress, out of sight of the Midianites. The angel of GOD appeared to him and said, "GOD is with you, O mighty warrior!"

Gideon replied, "With *me*, my master? If GOD is with us, why has all this happened to us? Where are all the miracle-wonders our parents and grandparents told us about, telling us, 'Didn't GOD deliver us from Egypt?' The fact is, GOD has nothing to do with us—he has turned us over to Midian."

But GOD faced him directly: "Go in this strength that is yours. Save Israel from Midian. Haven't I just sent you?"

Gideon said to him, "Me, my master? How and with what could I ever save Israel? Look at me. My clan's the weakest in Manasseh and I'm the runt of the litter."

GOD said to him, "I'll be with you. Believe me, you'll defeat Midian as one man."

JUDGES 6:11-16 (MESSAGE)

How the angel's greeting must have befuddled Gideon! This "mighty man of valor" was a nobody in his family, the members of his clan were insignificant in his tribe, his tribe wasn't anything to brag about, and Israel was being humiliated and oppressed under the thumb of the Midianites. If Gideon had felt that he was a mighty man of valor, would he have been beating out his wheat while hiding in the winepress?

Gideon was absolutely correct in his overall *appraisal* of the situation—he was by no means a person worthy of recognition, and his nation was in dire straits. Gideon, however, had a totally wrong *interpretation* of his life and circumstances. The problem, in so many ways, was that Gideon did not see himself in the same light that God saw him. There is perhaps no issue as important to daily living as our perspective of God's perspective of us.

How we believe God views us has a massive impact on not only our attitudes, but also the things we do and don't do. If, for some reason, we mistakenly consider God the Father to be a harsh drill sergeant just waiting to smack us when we mess up, we intuitively keep our distance. If we feel that others are more loved than we are, envy will sink its poisonous roots in our hearts. If we don't believe that God's favor shines upon us to meet our every need, we will always be hesitant to give generously to help others. If we fail to grasp our status as the highly honored children of the King, an extended wilderness season will leave us feeling as though God has dragged us out into a desolate place and left us there to die. The Christian faith will never work properly until we learn to see ourselves through heaven's eyes.

One of the great criticisms expressed toward the people in the Western church is that so many of us are apathetic—that we care little about the things of God and the moral decay of our world. Assuming that these judgments are accurate, what, we must ask, is the reason for such apathy? To be sure, there are professing Christians who are mostly self-absorbed and care little about others. This group, however, does not begin to constitute the sum total of all who appear to be apathetic. Could it be that a large number of us are convinced that who we are and what we do matters little?

Your average guy, for example, may feel backward and inept when it comes to religious matters. Failing to realize the glory and adventure involved with serving the King, he will pour his time and energy into work, hobbies, and watching sports—activities that he can either do well, or that make him feel good about who he is.

When that same man attends a Christian men's meeting, he will probably be bombarded with messages telling him how he needs to step up to the plate and be a man by fulfilling his responsibilities—obligations which include leading his family in areas he feels out of sync and ill-equipped to lead. In most cases, such a man will hesitate to give himself to spiritual matters in any significant way; therefore, we characterize him as apathetic. No, you can be sure that this guy has passion, but his enthusiasm will be directed only toward those arenas of life in which he feels confident, or in which he can feed off of the glory of others—such as viewing college or professional sports.

Was Gideon apathetic? From a distance, it may have appeared as though he cared little for anyone apart from himself. Still, I think that Gideon's problems had more to do with a lack of confidence than with emotional indifference. Because he failed to see himself through the eyes of heaven, Gideon had no comprehension of the amazing things God could do—and would do—through his seemingly insignificant life.

Is there something within your heart that yearns to make a profound impact in this world? Greatness isn't about having phenomenal abilities to rise above the crowd. At the heart of true greatness beats a heart that cares about others. But empathy alone is never enough; we must also see ourselves through the eyes of the Holy Spirit who empowers us. What is the common denominator between all of the people who have powerfully touched our world? They believed that they could!

PROBING QUESTIONS

How can feeling powerless and insignificant paralyze a person?

Why do you think that men are so often resistant to get involved with Christianity?

What would you do differently if you had absolute confidence that God's mighty hand of favor was upon you?

ACTION STEP
Identify one key area of your life in which you are hiding in the shadows because you feel you are insignificant and can do nothing to make a difference.

CLOSING PRAYER
Lord, please help me to see myself as You see me. Cleanse any apathetic roots from my heart and awaken within me a passion for Your kingdom!

FURTHER READING
Exodus 4:1-18; 1 Samuel 16:1-13; Luke 1:5-20

CHAPTER FORTY-TWO
NOBODIES FOR JESUS

Those that God used in the past were just ordinary people with an extraordinary Master. They were not all champions of great faith, but little people who saw their own need, and put their small faith in a great God.

—Winkie Pratney, revivalist and author

Then Jerubbaal (that is, Gideon) and all the people who were with him rose early and encamped beside the spring of Harod. And the camp of Midian was north of them, by the hill of Moreh, in the valley.

The LORD said to Gideon, "The people with you are too many for me to give the Midianites into their hand, lest Israel boast over me, saying, 'My own hand has saved me.'"
JUDGES 7:1-2 (ESV)

The instant we begin to address the significance of our identity in the eyes of God, some Christian leaders grow nervous. Pride, they fear, will enter human hearts and create all sorts of chaos in their ministries. It isn't that leaders don't want people to realize their full potential, but that far too many have had to do damage control in the wake of a self-proclaimed—and self-absorbed—"anointed servant of God" who foolishly brandished "the sword of the Lord" without wisdom or compassion.

People are prone to extremes. At one end of the spectrum, we have some Christian teachers proclaiming that humans are "little gods". On the other end, leaders constantly berate their people as "unworthy sinners, weak worms in the dust" who would have no reason to live but for the unwarranted grace of God.

While we must strive to avoid anything that reeks of self-deification, keeping people miserable and feeling like they are worthless is comparable to sedating them with drugs. (Keeping a person feeling worthless can actually lead to a need for anti-depressants!) Isn't this how we approach most mental illnesses? Diagnosing the problem may not be all that difficult. The cure, however, eludes our grasp. The next best thing, then, is to keep an unstable person in a drug-induced stupor in order to protect him and the rest of society from harm.

I never played much organized baseball, but I always did my best to support my son, Mike, in his athletic endeavors. As it is with many parents, attending Little League baseball games became a rite of passage of sorts. Over time, I noticed a common occurrence. A young pitcher would be throwing the ball high and out of the strike zone. Before long, the coaches would shout, "Get the ball down!" Almost without fail, the little guy would throw the next pitch into the dirt—still out of the strike zone. Such was to be expected with young players who had not yet matured in their abilities.

The way to combat error in the church is not to overreact with the opposite error. No. Those who wish to produce mature and fruitful disciples of Christ must learn to zero in on the truth. We dare not foster unbelief to correct errors in faith teaching, nor should we try to disarm pride by compelling people to continually grovel in the misery of their sinful tendencies.

Without question, pride is the archenemy of the human race, but the Creator of our souls is quite adept at accomplishing His objectives through His willing servants. It is for this very reason that God often—but not always—uses people who are virtual nobodies to carry out His awesome plans and purposes.

For look at your own calling as Christians, my brothers. You don't see among you many of the wise (according to this world's judgment) nor many of the ruling class, nor many from the noblest families. But God has chosen what the world calls foolish to shame the wise; he has chosen what the world calls weak to shame the strong. He has chosen things of little strength and small repute, yes and even things which have no real existence to explode the pretensions of the things that are— that no man may boast in the presence of God. Yet from this same God you have received your standing in Jesus Christ, and he has become for us the true wisdom, a matter, in practice, of being made righteous and holy, in fact, of being redeemed. And this makes us see the truth of scripture: "He who glories, let him glory in the Lord." 1 Corinthians 1:26-31 (Phillips)

Should we be surprised when heaven comes knocking at our door? In order to keep pride from doing its deadly damage, the all-knowing God delights to use insignificant people while fulfilling awesome ends. Humility, therefore, is indispensable.

But what is humility? Though we sometimes grapple to define this virtue, I can tell you what it is not. Humility is not a constant inward focus as we miserably berate ourselves. Is it humble to say "I am a worthless nobody," when God calls me a somebody in His eyes? Not in the least! If my perspective of myself disagrees with God, then I make Him to be a liar, which, we all should know, He cannot be.

Once again, we return to the importance of defining our identities as the covenant children of God. Apart from Him, living according to our own wisdom and ways, we are indeed miserable, weak, worm-infested sinners. We dare not forget this reality: We were drowning in a sea of sin, but God saved us and elevated us to the status of His royal sons and daughters. Does this give us grounds to boast? Only to the same degree that a drowning person brags about being saved as he was about to slip under the surface of the water for the last time!

Through the grace of God, we are *in* Christ. This reality now establishes us as new creations in the eyes of God. If we, who are foolish, weak, of little strength, of small repute, and have no real existence, are to ever play a significant role in turning the tide of evil in our world, we can no longer define ourselves according to who we were before we met our Savior. May heaven help us to clearly see ourselves through the lens of our Father's amazing favor!

PROBING QUESTIONS
How do you believe God views you? Does your perspective line up with what the Bible teaches?

Why does God so often work through people who are nobodies in the eyes of the world?

In what ways can a constant focus on our sins and inadequacies feed rather than hinder pride?

ACTION STEP
Take some time to redefine a despised weakness in your life as an opportunity for you to be humbly used by God for His eternal purposes.

CLOSING PRAYER
Father, I thank You so much that I don't need a worldly pedigree in order to make a significant impact in this world!

FURTHER READING
1 Corinthians 15:1-10; 2 Corinthians 5:16-21; Ephesians 2:1-10

CHAPTER FORTY-THREE
EXTREME FAVOR

*It is a fact of Christian experience that life is a series of troughs
and peaks. In His efforts to get permanent possession of the soul,
God relies on the troughs more than the peaks. And some of His
special favorites have gone through longer and deeper troughs
than anyone else.*
　　　　　　　　–Peter Marshall, pastor and chaplain to the U.S. Senate

---

**So, on the next day when Agrippa came together with
Bernice amid great pomp, and entered the auditorium
accompanied by the commanders and the prominent men
of the city, at the command of Festus, Paul was brought in.**
ACTS 25:23 (NASB)

**"King Agrippa, do you believe the Prophets? I know that
you do." Agrippa replied to Paul, "In a short time you will
persuade me to become a Christian." And Paul said, "I
would wish to God, that whether in a short or long time, not
only you, but also all who hear me this day, might become
such as I am, except for these chains."**
ACTS 26:27-30 (NASB)

Do you feel as though you are favored by God? What are your criteria
for thinking this way? Do you have (or lack) a great family? A body
to die for? Innate talents and abilities? More than a thousand social
media friends? A fantastic career? Loads of money in the bank?
Material possessions worthy of envy? Deceived is the person whose

perspective of God's favor depends upon outward appearances, or material possessions.

Contrast, if you will, the Apostle Paul with King Agrippa (II) and his sister, Bernice. Agrippa and Bernice had been born into royalty; their great grandfather was Herod the Great. This fabulously wealthy family managed to garner extensive favor with the Roman emperors. To ice the cake, Agrippa was given supreme power over the Jewish state.

Paul, on the other hand, was a prisoner, probably chained to a Roman guard. He must have been a sight to see, having received numerous beatings for his Christian faith. This once prominent Pharisee had given up everything to follow a new and strange religion. Further still, because of intense hatred by the masses, and more than one imprisonment, Paul was eventually abandoned by most of his companions. Based on his circumstances, it appeared that God had abandoned him as well. In the eyes of the world, Paul was a supreme loser. But who do you think was more favored by God?

The historian Josephus recorded that Agrippa and Bernice had a secret, incestuous relationship at one point in time.[5] Twice widowed, Bernice then married and deserted the King of Celicia, eventually becoming the mistress of the Roman emperor Titus. Also, Agrippa largely abandoned his Jewish faith to gain the wealth and power of Rome.

A snapshot of Paul's circumstances might have left a casual observer feeling pity for the poor guy. And yet, Paul was honored to play a crucial role not only in helping to establish the church, but also by penning an entire one-third of the New Testament. Billions of lives have been deeply touched by Paul's less than envious existence. Paul was highly favored by God. Agrippa and Bernice were not. But that is not the way that things appeared.

Why should any of this matter to us? How much time do we spend wishing that we had what others have? And how does such envy enhance our happiness? We still have an abundance of wealth in our nation and yet we live in misery as though we were cursed. I am not an advocate of poverty, nor do I believe that material possessions are totally unimportant. I am saying, however, that these things pale in importance when compared to the true, eternal blessings of God (see Ephesians 1). Envy will sap the very life from us.

The favor of God may be, at times, intangible, but it is no less real than the material world surrounding us. When the sovereign King of the Universe smiles upon us, what will we lack? Those who are favored by heaven can trust that their every need will be met in its appropriate time.

God's favor is in no way dependent upon one's appearance, performance, personal charm, or childhood circumstances. Nor does God's favor come to us by our own merit, but rather through Christ's substitutionary sacrifice on the cross. When we enter into a covenant relationship with God the Father through faith in Christ, we are blessed with the *very same* measure of favor He bestowed upon His Son.

This, however, is one case in which a simple nod of agreement cannot possibly suffice. In order to thoroughly defeat the destructive force of envy and its far reaching effects, our hearts must be totally convinced that our Father's favor shines brightly over our lives—even when outward circumstances scream the opposite. Until we learn to recognize and celebrate His favor, it is unlikely that our faith will ever flourish.

Personally, I have taken to regularly thanking my heavenly Father for His *Extreme Favor* in my life, doing my best to focus on the reality of the spiritual riches He has so graciously entrusted to me. The resulting impact has been nothing short of profound. God's *Extreme Favor*, when appropriated by faith in Christ, will manifest through all manner of unforeseen blessings. We never know exactly how God's blessings will come but we can be sure that our faithful Father will never abandon His beloved children.

Those who desire to see and experience the full expression of His favor will cleanse their hearts from sin (1 John 1:9) and vigorously guard their minds from selfish thinking. Learning to view life from God's vantage point opens up broad, new horizons right before our very eyes.

PROBING QUESTIONS

Why do we tend to limit our perspective of God's favor to outward appearances and material prosperity?

Is there an area of your life in which you have allowed envy to take root?

How does an envious heart serve to darken our view of life?

ACTION STEP

Set aside five minutes each day over the next week to verbally thank God for His favor on your life.

CLOSING PRAYER

Heavenly Father, I thank You so much for the *Extreme Favor* that You have extended to me through the cross of Jesus Christ. Please help the reality of that favor to permeate every fiber of my being!

FURTHER READING

Romans 8:26-39; Ephesians 1; James 3:13-18

CHAPTER FORTY-FOUR

PAY NO ATTENTION TO HARLEY AND REX

Popularity has slain more prophets of God than persecution ever did.

–Vance Havner, preacher and author

When Ahab saw Elijah, Ahab said to him, "Is it you, you troubler of Israel?" And he answered, "I have not troubled Israel, but you have, and your father's house, because you have abandoned the commandments of the LORD and followed the Baals."

1 KINGS 18:17-18 (ESV)

Debi and I live in a pet-friendly neighborhood where cats and dogs abound. Directly adjacent to our property, on the other side of a large fence, live Harley, Rex, and Cody. Now getting up in years, Cody, a Black Lab, is mostly quiet. Harley, a German Shepherd, and Rex, a mutt, are another story. When Harley and Rex spy me out working in my garden, or cooking on the grill, they go crazy—Rex baying with his loud, deep bark and Harley with his sharp, explosive voice of displeasure.

The problem for Harley and Rex is that, in spite of their territorial objections to my presence, I am on my own property for which I can produce a deed of ownership. Neither Harley nor Rex could do the same—not that they would care a dog's treat about legal ownership of property. From their territorial, tunnel-vision dog-perspective, what they see is what they own.

Have you ever felt like you don't belong? That you just don't fit in? Do you hear unfriendly voices loudly barking that you are unwelcome? If you seek to walk with God, being out of sync with this world's standards is unavoidable.

But what if you struggle to fit in with the people of God? Perhaps you are devoted to prayer while those around you focus on being entertained. Or maybe you have an intense passion for evangelism but nobody seems to care. Just about any God-given passion might produce similar results when others fail to share our enthusiasm.

Another side of the out-of-sync coin may be that you feel as though you live a subpar Christian existence in the midst of spiritual all-stars. They pray so eloquently and speak so fluently; surely they must touch spiritual heights with their every prayer.

It's all too easy to center our focus on how we don't fit, magnifying each agonizing detail by which we think we fall short. Such a sense of not belonging can produce a wilderness experience within itself. Striving to make oneself fit, however, may only make matters worse. In the end, we can isolate ourselves from God—a sacrifice far too costly for a few grains of human (or neighborhood dog) approval.

I tend to see a subtle and yet powerful difference between *fitting in* and *belonging*. Just because I don't fit in with Harley and Rex doesn't mean that I don't belong in my own yard. Indeed, in spite of their loud objections, I have a legal right to mow my yard, tend my garden, or cook my venison steaks. It is my yard. I belong there.

Elijah's experience was not unique—there will always be voices that attempt to banish us into a wilderness of isolation. Sometimes those voices proceed from those around us—classmates, coworkers, unfriendly neighbors, etc. There are, however, other times when the call for our banishment comes from within our own minds—those nagging, internal voices telling us that we don't belong.

Regardless of the source of the voice, this issue must first and foremost be settled between us and God. These internal struggles ultimately come not from the rejection of others, but from our own uncertainty of our identity in the eyes of God. When we begin to plumb the depths of our covenant relationship with the King of kings and Lord of lords—the Ruler of the Universe—those other voices matter little and the issue of fitting in becomes secondary. If you feel the need to belong, let it first be fulfilled through your perspective of God's perspective of you.

Those who have entered fully into the New Covenant with Christ can know with confidence that they belong, that they have been called, that they have been chosen, that they have been accepted, that they have been appointed to courageously serve God's purposes and proclaim His name to their generation. And what if Harley and Rex begin to bark? Simply wave, wish them a good day, and be about your Father's business. You may not fit in, but as a covenant child of heaven's King, you belong!

PROBING QUESTIONS

What is the difference between *fitting in* and *belonging*?

Can you list a few of the voices over the years that have attempted to banish you into a wilderness of isolation?

How does knowing our identity in the eyes of God help lay the foundation for knowing that we belong?

ACTION STEP

Identify any areas of your life in which you may have permitted loud voices like those of Harley and Rex to intimidate you. Spend some time considering how a covenant child of the King should respond to those voices.

CLOSING PRAYER

Heavenly Father, thank You so much for choosing me as Your child! Please help the reality of this identity to permeate every fiber of my being.

FURTHER READING

John 1:10-13; Galatians 4:1-7; 1 Peter 1:1-12

CHAPTER FORTY-FIVE
IT'S NOT JUST ABOUT YOU

You will have no test of faith that will not fit you to be a blessing if you are obedient to the Lord. I never had a trial but when I got out of the deep river I found some poor pilgrim on the bank that I was able to help by that very experience.
                    –A.B. Simpson, evangelist and church founder

---

But Joseph said to them, "Do not be afraid, for am I in God's place? As for you, you meant evil against me, but God meant it for good in order to bring about this present result, to preserve many people alive. So therefore, do not be afraid; I will provide for you and your little ones." So he comforted them and spoke kindly to them.
                    GENESIS 50:19-21 (NASB)

God wants to do something great *through* us, not just *for* us. The very thought strikes a chord of hope in our hearts! Joseph's wilderness experience preserved not only the lives of his family—including the lineage of Christ—but also a multitude throughout the entire region. Moses led his people out of bondage in Egypt and set the stage for succeeding generations to dwell in the Promised Land. Through intense opposition and suffering, Paul penned one-third of the New Testament, serving as a source of life and inspiration for billions. And what more can we say about Jesus? After being tempted by the devil in the wilderness, the Messiah went on to make the most significant mark of any person ever to walk the face of this earth.

During difficult, isolated seasons, we are tempted to think primarily about ourselves. We wonder if God has perhaps abandoned us. We focus on the wrongs inflicted by others. We wallow and stew, unable to make any real sense of what appears to be an unjust existence. But what if? What if God was up to something greater, a marvelous work transcending our natural ability to see?

I have always been a believer in the free will of humankind, convinced that God allows us to make our own choices for which we bear the fruit, either good or bad. At the same time, I have come to understand that our human freedoms can be expressed only under the umbrella of our Creator's sovereignty. Nothing happens that He doesn't allow, and in the end He somehow manages to steer our free choices toward His sovereign purposes—something far more amazing than if He were a giant puppeteer in heaven. This, in one sense, is what makes Him God.

I do not, however, like the popular phrase, "God is in control." We see plenty of death and destruction in our world that all run contrary to God's nature as the author and giver of life. We would do better, in my opinion, to proclaim along with the Scriptures, "God reigns!" He is—and always will be—the ultimate authority in the Universe who will one day call to account every thought, word, and deed.

We can draw great comfort and encouragement from the scriptural promise that "God causes all things to work together for good to those who love God, to those who are called according to His purpose" (Romans 8:28). As we take the time to consider this promise, we can't help but realize its unique nature. No matter what we go through, no matter how painful the journey, or how horrible the experience, our Heavenly Father promises to work it all out for our greater benefit. And what is our greater benefit? That we would "become conformed to the image of His Son" (Romans 8:29).

Only minimal effort is required to recognize that an integral aspect of Christ's character is His love for others. It wasn't for His own benefit that Jesus fasted in the desert for forty days; our Lord and Savior paid a huge price for the sake of others. If we are to be conformed into Christ's glorious image, then it is entirely reasonable that a primary purpose for such a transformation would be to benefit someone other than ourselves.

Through the years, I have observed that God is not especially efficient with His use of time—never does He run on a Western schedule. God-ordained wilderness experiences can go on for years. However, our Lord does appear to be quite effective with His use of the trials and tribulations that we experience in this broken world— even when they do not make sense to us.

When Debi and I began doing campus ministry, our initial twenty-one months were frustrating, painful, and visibly unproductive. The several years that followed weren't much to brag about either. Throughout that long season of struggle, we often wondered what had happened to the promises we felt God had given us. In time, we did see a measure of success and I eventually found myself coaching other campus ministers. Please don't miss the importance of this fact: I soon discovered that I had been through just about every struggle they were experiencing. I was elated (and somewhat relieved) to see the powerful effects that my victories over my previous struggles were having on their lives and ministries. It was something I never could have foreseen; the full picture came together only as I entered that new phase of service.

The day you became a Christian was the day you gave—or should have given—God the freedom to write the story of your life, to use you for His good pleasure, to accomplish His plans and purposes in His good time. Yes, it is essential that you grasp His extreme love for you, possessing the acute awareness that you are always in His thoughts, but don't be fooled into believing that your difficulties are only about you. Remember, your God wants to do something great *through* you, not just *for* you. Your wilderness journey, when aligned with the dynamics of God's eternal kingdom, will produce succulent fruit from which a multitude of others will feast!

PROBING QUESTIONS

What is the difference between God *reigning* over the universe and God *controlling* everything that happens?

What does it mean to say that, "God causes all things to work together for good" (Romans 8:28-29)?

Can you recall a time when your difficulties made sense only after they had served to help another person?

ACTION STEP
Think about your most challenging struggle and consider ways that God may one day use it to help someone else.

CLOSING PRAYER
Lord, please forgive my self-centeredness. I surrender myself fully to Your good plans and purposes, asking that You would use my difficulties to bless others in ways beyond what I can imagine.

FURTHER READING
Genesis 50:1-21; Psalms 146; Romans 8:28-29; 1 Corinthians 9:19-23

CHAPTER FORTY-SIX
JESUS, OF COURSE, WAS RIGHT

Apart from one trite exception, the entire world consists of others.
–Source Unknown

Now the LORD said to Abram, "Go from your country and your kindred and your father's house to the land that I will show you. And I will make of you a great nation, and I will bless you and make your name great, so that you will be a blessing. I will bless those who bless you, and him who dishonors you I will curse, and in you all the families of the earth shall be blessed."

GENESIS 12:1-3 (ESV)

The evening was painful and exhausting! Debi and I had organized one of several dinner events for our church, but for some unknown reason, this endeavor was in many ways a disaster. Our volunteer kitchen helpers clashed with one another all evening, some people's kids ran wild, and our own small children, who were usually very compliant in public, chose that particular evening to break from their usual pattern and be difficult.

After finally completing the tortuous clean-up, my spouse and I collapsed into the front seats of our car, staring at the newly inscribed lines of exhaustion that now marked each other's tired faces. "Is this really worth it?" was our question as we sat for a few minutes and pondered the value of our labors. Simultaneously, we each responded with the same answer: "Yes, the evening was worth the effort!" Anything we could do for Christ, we concluded, was nothing in comparison to what He had done for us. He was worthy, we affirmed, of receiving all that we could give—and more.

Jesus once said, "It is more blessed to give than to receive" (see Acts 20:35), but I don't think many of us actually believe these words. If we truly thought giving to be more blessed than receiving, there would be many more givers than consumers in our churches and in our society as a whole. A simple survey of our cultural landscape shows the exact opposite. To make matters worse, we aren't just receivers; in many cases we are takers, often going to extreme lengths to ensure that we get what we think we deserve.

I think that many people possess a romanticized vision of what it means to give, but the picture easily turns sour when giving comes with a price greater than expected. It is like the time we found a stray dog wandering in our neighborhood. Afraid that it would be hit by a car, I grabbed a leash and began to canvas the surrounding neighborhood in search of its home. Two hours later, I found the semi-grateful owner; the experience had vaporized my morning devotional plans. Nice thought, difficult fulfillment. All of us can probably recall experiences in which the notion of lending a helping hand became painfully difficult, causing us to think cautiously about any future generosity.

When God spoke promises of greatness and blessing to Abram, He deliberately included the idea that Abram himself would be a blessing to others. We prefer to overlook this particular element of favor, but cannot do so without destroying the heart of the matter.

In heaven's eyes, greatness, as defined by humanity, isn't greatness at all. Those who boast of their abilities and possessions may garner human admiration, but they will certainly lack heaven's favor. Through the lens of heaven, true greatness is never self-centered. No, the virtues that rivet God's attention are humility and selfless love. Kingdom-defined greatness possesses an eternal quality—it lasts and lasts and lasts well beyond what we can imagine. In contrast, human glory is short lived. The athletic hero in one game may find himself to be the goat in the next, his previous exploits being quickly forgotten.

When I take the time to consider what has been most meaningful about my life, the answer is never the things I own, or the worldly successes I have achieved. I spent seventeen years of my life working for a large coal company, earning a management position and a respectable salary. That period was followed by ten years of relatively low income as a campus minister. But to me, there is no comparison; in spite of the many sacrifices involved, my years working with college students carry so much more significance. True meaning always involves an investment in others, and such investments never fail to exact a price.

What is it that enables us to be characterized as givers in this life? I would say it is personally knowing our heavenly Father and having the confidence that we are His much-loved children. Our Father, by His very nature, is the epitome of giving, having set the all-time standard by sending His much-loved Son as a sacrifice for our sins. Further still, He will provide for our every need as we give of ourselves to others in obedience to His leading.

As we give to honor God, the responses of those we serve become secondary in nature. Our heavenly Father remembers our loving generosity regardless of what any human thinks. Even more, anonymous giving catches God's eye because fewer selfish motives can be attached.

I fully understand that our world is full of selfish consumers and that we must give wisely; therefore, following the Holy Spirit's leading is essential. Giving should not simply be a matter of conscience, lest we find ourselves manipulated by those who prey upon guilt and emotion. But when we walk in the steps preordained by our Creator, lovingly doing the works that He has prepared since before the foundation of the world (see Ephesians 2:10), our giving will both honor God and return untold blessings upon our own heads. Champions of the faith understand these things and will continue to glorify their Lord and Savior by giving sacrificially even through difficult times. *Jesus, of Course, Was Right*; it really is more blessed to give than to receive!

PROBING QUESTIONS

Explain why it is more blessed to give than to receive. Do you truly believe the explanation you just gave?

Why is giving anonymously so difficult for us?

Why must true greatness always be other-centered?

ACTION STEP
Prayerfully formulate a loosely structured plan to honor God by wisely giving of your time, energy, and money.

CLOSING PRAYER
Father, I thank You so much for the gift of Your Son for my salvation! Please help me to know in the depths of my heart that it truly is better to give than to receive.

FURTHER READING
Matthew 6:1-4; Luke 16:9-15; Acts 20:28-35; Hebrews 6:9-12

CHAPTER FORTY-SEVEN
DON'T GIVE UP ON THE CHURCH

If the Church is a living body united to the same head, governed by the same laws, and pervaded by the same Spirit, it is impossible that one part should be independent of all the rest.
—Charles Hodge, scholar and author

By faith Moses, when he had grown up, refused to be called the son of Pharaoh's daughter, choosing rather to endure ill-treatment with the people of God than to enjoy the passing pleasures of sin, considering the reproach of Christ greater riches than the treasures of Egypt; for he was looking to the reward.

HEBREWS 11:24-26 (NASB)

Many books have been written in recent years about the failure of the Western church. Bloggers publicly express their dissatisfaction. Mainstream media gloat as they air every piece of dirty laundry. Protesters boldly demean her old-fashioned ways. Today's mindset tells us that we can fully embrace Jesus while avoiding any type of organized religion, that we can embrace the church universal while never connecting with other believers on a local level.

When I speak of *a church*, I don't mean the physical building that we call a church. Such a building is actually a place where a church—*a local gathering of believers*—meets. In addition to local churches, we can also speak of *the church* as *the universal body of Christ*—the sum total of all who profess faith in Jesus. A local church is simply an expression of the body of Christ as a whole.

Many in Western society deduce that being part of the universal body of Christ need not include involvement on the local level. They can be Christians, they believe, without being connected to a local fellowship of believers. Such a perspective may be accurate to a point, but it betrays the very essence of New Covenant teaching.

Our love for God can only be adequately expressed as we live out a practical love for one another; and without one another we will never fully mature to be the people God has destined us to become. I don't think God cares much whether we participate in a traditional denominational church, or something more like a house church, as long as the life of God is present. What matters is that we corporately live out His love for us. It all comes down to being connected.

Anyone who has ever been involved in a local church can probably share at least one painful story of having been hurt by its members. The same could be said about any type of relational environment, but when it comes to churches, we expect something more. If people are truly following Christ, it stands to reason that they should reflect His love.

Allow me to be painfully honest and say that I believe much of today's criticism of the Western church is indeed justified. By their very nature, churches attract broken people. There will always be those individuals, I have learned, who connect with a church only to serve their own interests; they have no intention or desire to grow. But even for those on the path of restoration, the process can be unpleasantly slow; selfish and immature behavior is inevitable.

We also face the difficulty of dealing with a church as an organization. Because people are broken, policies must be set in place. In addition, needs are often overwhelming, with pastors and other leaders still being subject to their own human limitations. They face a very real temptation, if not pressure, to try to do ministry without taking the time to continually cultivate their own walk with God.

Not long ago, people tended to stay with a church even if they didn't like it. It was the loyal thing to do. Pastors and priests were put on pedestals higher than their preaching platforms; congregants respected their authority and integrity. Much has changed in recent years, and some of it is the church's own fault. Covering up child molestation, for example, rings of hypocrisy, going directly against all that Jesus lived and died to accomplish.

Debi and I have been members of the same church since 1984 and during that time we have experienced firsthand the selfish and callous behavior of human nature. Personally, I have been financially cheated, unjustly accused, and unfairly abandoned. (Dare I mention my own failures as well?) I also co-labored in ministry (outside of our church) for several years with a man whose life was little more than a bold-faced lie, leaving me devastated when the truth finally surfaced. If I chose to dwell on the hurts, I could fill a book with the gory details of all of my negative experiences.

Why have we stayed involved with our local church and with Christian ministry through all of these years? The reasons for staying connected are far more numerous than the offenses we've experienced. We have longstanding friendships that we value highly. Our lives have been enriched much more than they have been damaged. In fact, each and every one of our negative experiences has helped us to mature as overcomers in Christ; branches of spiritual growth often flourish in the midst of relational challenges. And, most importantly, we love the church because Jesus loves the church. She is His passion to the point of being treated as His *bride* (2 Corinthians 11:2; Ephesians 5:25-27). Because we love Him, we will never stop seeking her welfare.

Those who have been hurt by the people of God (or nicely dressed imposters) do not stand alone. Moses paid a similar price of ill-treatment, and yet, through the eye of faith, he recognized a glory greater than any measure of human brokenness. Under the New Covenant, we have something greater still. Even in the midst of relational struggles, the potential for richness runs deep. Many a wilderness season can be put behind us simply by connecting to a healthy local expression of the body of Christ.

I freely admit that in seeking out a local expression of the church, we must choose prayerfully and wisely. (Appendix III is intended to help you with this process.) The intent is to connect with a life-filled body of believing Christians—not a local expression of *Stagnant Waters Church* or *Abundant Rules Nonfellowship*.

A sparkling treasure of the wilderness is the realization that, as Christians, we are all in this together, that each is a weak vessel seeking to honor God in spite of our human propensity to sin. Regardless of any current (or recurrent) imperfections on her part, Christ has not abandoned His bride—and neither should we.

PROBING QUESTIONS

Are you involved in some type of local body of believers? Why or why not?

Why is it important to choose a church wisely?

Under what circumstances should a person leave a church? How can this be done in a way that honors God?

ACTION STEP

If you are currently connected with a local church, take some time to deliberately forgive anyone who has hurt you. (Follow through with a conversation if needed.) If you are not connected, please read Appendix III.

CLOSING PRAYER

Jesus, please open my eyes to Your love for Your church. I want to value what You value!

FURTHER READING

Romans 12; 1 Corinthians 12:12-27; Ephesians 4:11-16

CHAPTER FORTY-EIGHT
AIM OR COMPLAIN

Those who complain most are most to be complained of.
–Matthew Henry, pastor and author

For I do not want you to be unaware, brethren, that our fathers were all under the cloud and all passed through the sea; and all were baptized into Moses in the cloud and in the sea; and all ate the same spiritual food; and all drank the same spiritual drink, for they were drinking from a spiritual rock which followed them; and the rock was Christ. Nevertheless, with most of them God was not well-pleased; for they were laid low in the wilderness. Now these things happened as examples for us, so that we would not crave evil things as they also craved. . . . Nor grumble, as some of them did, and were destroyed by the destroyer.
1 CORINTHIANS 10:1-6, 10 (NASB)

Several years ago, I read an update from a popular ministry that railed about a certain judge who was antagonistic toward our faith. He even went so far as to call evangelical Christians a bunch of "whiners and complainers." I suppose that the appropriate Christian response would have been outrage toward that audacious man, but in considering the statement, I sadly realized that his generalization was all too accurate. Ironically, the fact that they were complaining about the judge more or less validated his point.

Now don't get me wrong—I am not supporting anti-God policies! And trust me—I know all too well that the "whine potential" in our country increases on a daily basis. There is a lot to be upset about! At the same time, the world is simply being the world, with people saying and doing what Jesus predicted they would say and do.

Early Christians had a very different perspective of persecution and other difficulties related to bearing the name of Christ. Paul and Silas, for example, sang praises to God in the middle of the night as they sat chained in a miserable, stench-filled, rat-infested dungeon (Acts 16:22-26). Paul's personality was anything but passive and yet he later spoke of a secret that enabled him to remain content in the midst of each and every circumstance.

> *Not that I speak from want, for I have learned to be content in whatever circumstances I am. I know how to get along with humble means, and I also know how to live in prosperity; in any and every circumstance I have learned the secret of being filled and going hungry, both of having abundance and suffering need. I can do all things through Him who strengthens me.* Philippians 4:11-13 (NASB)

Christians routinely quote the latter part of this passage but rarely within its original context of contentment. I think, in part, that is because we are not content, do not understand contentment, and do not grasp the nature of Paul's secret.

Contentment is not a passive, fatalistic attitude that resigns itself to thinking whatever is going to happen is going to happen. Paul was not content with errant Christianity, or with people not knowing Christ—as evidenced by his aggressive witness and sacrificial lifestyle. Paul, however, was saying that He had learned the secret of being at rest regardless of whether his personal circumstances were favorable or adverse.

What was Paul's secret? He recognized that every circumstance, whether good or bad, pleasant or painful, just or unjust, provided him with an opportunity to *identify* with Christ. Through His earthly life and subsequent death on the cross, Jesus experienced it all—every form of human suffering. And to be identified with Christ, well, there is no greater honor—no matter what form that identification takes.

How changed are my ambitions! Now I long to know Christ and the power shown by his resurrection: now I long to share his sufferings, even to die as he died, so that I may perhaps attain as he did, the resurrection from the dead. Philippians 3:10-11 (Phillips)

Of course, we all want to share in the fullness of God's blessings, but do we aim to know Him to the degree that we consider it an honor to share in His sufferings? It seems to me that we either aim to know Him and all that entails, or we complain about a world that is becoming increasingly unlike what we want.

Ours is a crucial time in history for the church as God uses adverse circumstances to separate the *wheat* from the *chaff* (see Matthew 3:12). Few things do as much to distinguish the true people of God from those mired in worldly mindsets than how we respond to circumstances that are not according to our liking.

The wilderness generation of Israelites never learned this secret, failing to comprehend the amazing opportunity they had been given to be identified as the people of the God of Abraham, Isaac, and Jacob. Their negative example is one we dare not follow. At some point, we must ask ourselves if we truly desire to know Him, or if we just want the benefits that come with having God in our lives. If we aim to know Him and to be identified with Him in each and every way, our tendencies to complain will mysteriously begin to vanish.

To know Him—there is no higher call; to make Him known—no greater privilege; to identify with His name—no greater honor!

PROBING QUESTIONS

Why does complaining come so naturally for us?

Why is being identified with Christ the highest honor a person can know?

Do you truly desire to know Him or do you just want the benefits that come from having God in your life?

ACTION STEP

Identify a passage of Scripture that you can draw from to help your attitude when you are tempted to complain.

CLOSING PRAYER

Lord, please cleanse any ungratefulness from my heart and forgive any complaining attitude on my part. I want to aim to know You in all that I do and say.

FURTHER READING

Acts 5:17-42, 16:16-34; Philippians 2:14-16; Hebrews 4:14-16

CHAPTER FORTY-NINE
HOLY DISCONTENTMENT

Were there none who were discontented with what they have, the world would never reach anything better.
        –Florence Nightingale, humanitarian and writer

By faith he lived as an alien in the land of promise, as in a foreign land, dwelling in tents with Isaac and Jacob, fellow heirs of the same promise; for he was looking for the city which has foundations, whose architect and builder is God.
                                        HEBREWS 11:9-10 (NASB)

There I was—a few short months after coming to Christ—talking with John, an older man who looked as though his days on earth were nearing an end. My conscience was nagging me to share the gospel with this seemingly friendly man, but strangely enough, I felt a strong impression from the Holy Spirit that it would not be a good idea. Not sharing my faith went against everything I had been taught, so exercising a full measure of my own wisdom, I obeyed my conscience and ignored the Spirit's leading. What followed was a twenty to thirty-minute tirade by John about all that was wrong with the church he attended. Much of that conversation remains an unpleasant blur, but I do remember vehement statements to the effect that a sermon should never be longer than twenty minutes and that any church service lasting more than an hour was sure to offend high heaven.

It is an unfortunate reality; some people will always be dissatisfied regardless of how hard we try to please them. "Malcontent" is the word I would use to describe them. Whether we speak of the configuration of the parking lot, the color of the church carpeting, or the tone of the pastor, these people will always find something to complain about. Many also have a history of bouncing from church to church, wreaking havoc in whatever unfortunate fellowship they happen to land.

Sadly, those of us in leadership are often quick to label all who are discontent as being *malcontent*—meaning that anyone who isn't happy with our church or organization is probably *a self-absorbed complainer*. We use the Israelites' poor example in the wilderness to silence any and all rumblings of discontentment because, as God's anointed leaders, we are always right and those who challenge us are always wrong.

I can't pinpoint a specific time or incident, but one day the realization began to dawn on me that not all who are discontent are malcontent, that some of the most dissatisfied people in our world are those who care the most as they passionately search for God's kingdom. Perhaps these folks should be looking elsewhere, although it seems to me that a church is as good a place as any to be seeking out the dynamics of God's kingdom rule.

Although I don't have statistics to back me up, it appears that the number of people who are discontent with the Western church—for reasons both good and bad—is at an all-time high. And with trends differing from the past, many of these people have quit bouncing from church to church; they no longer participate in any local expression of the body of Christ. Instead, their pursuit of God is limited to personal devotions, religious broadcasting, or online sources. And while I certainly understand their frustration, regardless of their motives, the trends are less than healthy.

The truth is that life in this broken world rarely provides all that we hope for—even when our desires fully honor God. While many aspects of our negative circumstances may be beyond our control, it does fall upon us to decide how we will respond to those unfavorable situations. I believe, then, the question at hand is, "How do we process *Holy Discontentment*?"

No particular formula will fit our needs, for every person and every set of circumstances is different. Some may be called to relocate and others to stay, some to speak out and others to remain silent, some to cause a stir and others to patiently pray. There are, however, three virtues that have universal application for any situation.

The first virtue is faith. In spite of his adverse circumstances and the delay in seeing God's promise fulfilled, Abraham never became a cynical complainer. He lived by an enduring faith, which pleased God to no end.

No matter how dark a situation appears, frustration and despair serve no beneficial purposes. The truly Christian course of action is to look with objective honesty at any negative circumstance, and to believe that our God is willing and able to work powerfully—regardless of any human shortcomings. I have been in some very dark ministry situations which, I freely admit, I did not handle as well as I should have. And yet, somehow, through it all, God brought favorable changes to each of those situations. Still, the challenges would have been much less painful for me had I more effectively exercised a day by day trust in my Lord and Savior.

Second, love is essential no matter what we encounter. We all agree that love is powerful. We all desire to be loved. We all recognize that love is integral to the Christian faith. But when it comes to actually loving those who neglect or mistreat us, well, for some strange reason we feel justified to respond with bitter contempt. Such reactions serve as a powerful commentary on our human waywardness. Love, my friends, is never optional, and a hardened heart is certain to lead to a parched spirit.

Wisdom, our third virtue, is what enables us to effectively apply faith and love in any given situation. Without wisdom, our attempts at faith may amount to little more than ill-timed presumption, and our love can be dangerously misdirected.

Are you discontent? You may have just cause. Perhaps our gracious God has put eternity in your heart and given you the discernment to identify false or imperfect representations of His kingdom. But what will you do with what you see? Will you throw your hands in the air in disgust, or will you pray in faith? Will you become hard and cynical, or will you be a vessel of God's love? Will you resign yourself to doing nothing, or will you honor your King and help to redeem a world that will always be less than perfect? As Florence Nightingale so wisely stated, "Were there none who were discontented with what they have, the world would never reach anything better."

PROBING QUESTIONS

Are you mostly content, discontent, or malcontent?

What do you think is the best way to process discontentment?

Why is wisdom essential when applying faith and love to any given circumstance?

ACTION STEP

Have you allowed discontentment to turn you into a critical complainer? It may be a good idea to ask forgiveness of Christ, the head of the church, and of any people you may have hurt in the process.

CLOSING PRAYER

Lord God, please give me a vision for Your kingdom on earth and the wisdom to know how to help that vision become a reality.

FURTHER READING

Philippians 1:12-25, 2:12-18; James 3:13-18

CHAPTER FIFTY
THE STATUS IS NOT QUO

"Maybe Treebeard's right. We don't belong here, Merry. It's too big for us. What can we do in the end? We've got the Shire. Maybe we should go."

"The fires of Isengard will spread. And the woods of Tuckborough and Buckland will burn. And all that was once green and good in this world will be gone. There won't be a Shire, Pippin."
  –a conversation between Pippin and Merry in *The Two Towers* film adaptation of J.R.R. Tolkien's *The Lord of the Rings*

When they entered, he looked at Eliab and thought, "Surely the LORD'S anointed is before Him." But the LORD said to Samuel, "Do not look at his appearance or at the height of his stature, because I have rejected him; for God sees not as man sees, for man looks at the outward appearance, but the LORD looks at the heart." . . . Thus Jesse made seven of his sons pass before Samuel. But Samuel said to Jesse, "The LORD has not chosen these." And Samuel said to Jesse, "Are these all the children?" And he said, "There remains yet the youngest, and behold, he is tending the sheep." Then Samuel said to Jesse, "Send and bring him; for we will not sit down until he comes here." So he sent and brought him in. Now he was ruddy, with beautiful eyes and a handsome appearance. And the LORD said, "Arise, anoint him; for this is he."

1 SAMUEL 16:6-12 (NASB)

In J.R.R. Tolkien's world of fantasy, hobbits were often called "halflings" because of their small stature and fear of adversity. While men were bold and brave and fit for war, hobbits appeared to be insignificant in the grand scheme of life. However, in Tolkien's *The Lord of the Rings* trilogy, a hobbit by the name of Frodo Baggins was assigned the task of destroying a golden ring that had been forged by the evil Sauron to rule over all of Middle Earth. Because of— rather than in spite of—his small stature, Frodo succeeded where many gifted and well-trained warriors had failed. The book series is, of course, a work of fiction, but Tolkien, as a devout Christian, creatively used fantasy to effectively illustrate complicated spiritual truths. His books are pregnant with meaning!

The concept of a halfling corresponds to reality in the form of men and women who fail to measure up to human standards of genetic superiority. God does not limit Himself to work through only those who fall short of this world's standards, but He is in the habit of doing so. In fact, God delights in using "human halflings" to accomplish His grand purposes. Why? Those confident in their own wisdom and ability are readily prone to pride. A human halfling fully understands his or her limited ability, and therefore learns to effectively abide in the empowering grace of God. In the end, they accomplish feats of glory that far surpass anything humanly possible.

This all sounds great, but halflings have an inherent problem— they think small. Most halflings possess an innate mentality that only those of "full stature" can be champions for the kingdom of God. Halflings, then, tend to live in the world of shadows, pursuing a comfortable existence and avoiding unnecessary difficulties (and adventures). Their purpose (in their own eyes) is not to change the world, but to cheer on the gifted few. All too rare is the human halfling who understands that greatness is not found in the person, but in the great God who willingly empowers His people.

Picturing themselves as grasshoppers in a world of giants, those who fall short of this world's standards are particularly susceptible to fear and anxiety. David, however, was a halfling of a different caliber because he understood the nature of his covenant relationship with the Lord of hosts. In spite of his small stature and insignificant status,

David could not be content with the status quo; he desperately longed to see God's glory revealed through His people. Thus, a mere shepherd boy overcame impossible odds, displaying the courage of an emerging overcomer to become the most beloved king in Israel's history.

Perhaps this is where Tolkien's imagery is most powerful. That which is improbable—no, virtually impossible is a better term—can become reality because our God has destined us for victory. Those who truly love God cannot help but to move forward in service to our King. We must care (not simply to protect our self-interests) because God's heart is bound up in the welfare of humankind.

None of us are exempt to the call to advance God's kingdom. Whether we are large or small, strong or weak, gifted or lacking in talent, we are all members of God's mighty army. There is, however, one quality that we dare not lack and that is courage.

> *Therefore do not throw away your confidence, which has a great reward. For you have need of endurance, so that when you have done the will of God you may receive what is promised. For,*
> *"Yet a little while,*
> *and the coming one will come and will not delay;*
> *but my righteous one shall live by faith,*
> *and if he shrinks back,*
> *my soul has no pleasure in him."*
> *But we are not of those who shrink back and are destroyed, but of those who have faith and preserve their souls.* Hebrews 10:35-39 (ESV)

Is this to say that we will never be afraid? Absolutely not! And yet, we must squarely face our fears, which will eventually buckle under the weight of God's love. We fight in a life and death struggle between the kingdoms of light and darkness; we dare not attempt to avoid the conflict by hiding in our own personal Shire. And while final victory is assured for the kingdom of God, exactly who ends up on which side matters a great deal. Our call, then, is to courageously move forward, even as dark storm clouds gather, step by faltering step. When we live in obedience to our sovereign King, He will always make a way where there is no way, forever extending abundant grace to His emerging overcomers.

PROBING QUESTIONS
Historically, have you seen yourself as a "wholeling", or a "halfling"? Regardless of how you see yourself, why is humility so important for those who seek to be used for God's purposes?

Why are halflings especially dangerous against the forces of evil?

Why is being "small in stature" never a valid excuse from shrinking back in fear from God's purposes?

ACTION STEP
Identify an area of life in which God has burdened you, but in which you have failed to act because you see yourself as insignificant.

CLOSING PRAYER
Lord, please help my unbelief and enable me to live as a person of courage.

FURTHER READING
Joshua 1:1-9; Matthew 25:14-30; Hebrews 10:32-39

CHAPTER FIFTY-ONE
WILL YOU SHINE IN THE END TIMES?

God is preparing His heroes. And when the opportunity comes,
He can fit them into their places in a moment. And the world will
wonder where they came from.
—A.B. Simpson, evangelist and church founder

"Now at that time Michael, the great prince who stands guard over the sons of your people, will arise. And there will be a time of distress such as never occurred since there was a nation until that time; and at that time your people, everyone who is found written in the book, will be rescued. Many of those who sleep in the dust of the ground will awake, these to everlasting life, but the others to disgrace and everlasting contempt. Those who have insight will shine brightly like the brightness of the expanse of heaven, and those who lead the many to righteousness, like the stars forever and ever."

DANIEL 12:1-3 (NASB)

From my earliest days as a Christian, I admired Daniel as one of the premier personalities of the Bible. Somehow, this humble leader was able to conduct himself with wisdom, faithfulness, and courage through all of his days—even under the demands of the Mosaic Law and the dominions of idolatrous kings. Through the years, I have come to realize that the book of Daniel also serves as a handbook of sorts for those of us who must navigate the often desolate wilderness of the end times.

Daniel had been born into the privilege of royalty, but his unsettled times were nothing to be envied. The glory days of a unified and prosperous Jewish kingdom had long since passed, lingering now as only a wishful memory. About a hundred years prior to Daniel's birth, the Northern Kingdom of Israel had been conquered and essentially destroyed because of their persistent worship of false gods. The Southern Kingdom, Judah, continued to flip-flop between righteousness and idolatry, depending upon which king happened to be in power at the time. Josiah—a righteous man of integrity and zeal who instituted major reforms in an attempt to restore the glory days of Judah—served as king at the time Daniel was born.

I imagine Daniel's childhood as being filled with hope, but everything quickly unraveled when Josiah was killed in battle against Egypt. This led first to oppression and heavy taxation by Pharaoh Neco of Egypt, and then to total domination by the nation of Babylon. Daniel and his friends were exiled to Babylon, only to watch the final destruction of Judah from a distance. Worse still, they were soon forced to serve as administrators for King Nebuchadnezzar—the very despot who had plundered and destroyed their beloved homeland.

In spite of crazy times and the upheaval of kingdoms, Daniel faithfully walked with God in the midst of constant temptation, stayed true to his Lord despite intense pressure to worship other gods, and faithfully served several kings while surrounded by political enemies. Daniel's sensitive witness of humility, competency, and faithful service was so powerful that we may someday see one or more of those kings in heaven. At the very least, his faithful example gave other Jews the courage to stand strong for their faith through temptation and even persecution.

How did Daniel do all of this? He knew his righteous standing in the eyes of God and persistently sought to understand the dynamics of God's coming kingdom. When all looked hopeless and lost, Daniel continuously looked up, studying the Scriptures and taking time from his busy schedule to seek God in prayer three times each day. Dwelling in a wilderness of exile through an almost continuous onslaught of bad news, Daniel walked in steadfast faith, which in turn led to his faithful service to his Lord.

Can we draw a few parallels to our day? The world around us is a materialistic Babylon, overflowing with temptations of all sorts. The church of Jesus Christ finds itself under siege by intense persecution in many parts of the globe and lukewarm belief in others. Christians of all sorts face constant discouragement as they see days of glory fading into the realm of legend. As in the time of Daniel, it appears as though God has abandoned His wayward people.

Appearances, my friends, are often deceiving. The glory days of God's kingdom lie not in the past, but in the future. And the tumult we see in our world? It is the result of a sovereign shaking intended by God to separate the worthless from that which is truly and eternally valuable. Ours is a day for hope, not discouragement and despair.

Why must we be faithful to grasp and apply the concepts presented in this book? Because true glory lies before us as God prepares a generation of leaders who will guide many to eternal righteousness. But in order to lead others along this noble path, we must first grasp the nature of true righteousness ourselves. Yes, we need to exercise absolute faith in our Lord and Savior, and yes, we should come to fully understand our status as the sons and daughters of the King. At the same time, we would do well to follow the examples set by Daniel and the Apostle Paul in taking the attitude of humble bond-servants.

History reveals seasons in which God gifted generations of believers to powerfully advance His kingdom purposes. However, one need study only a smattering of church history to realize that far too many Christian movements have succumbed to the subtle and incessant temptation of human pride. In modern times, the quest for human glory within the church has left us in a severely weakened and relatively ineffective state. Still, I believe that God is preparing a generation of halflings whom He will mightily use to advance His eternal purposes in these last days. If God raises up big-name leaders, it is only for the purpose of serving and equipping a generation of faithful believers, not to form personality cults revolving around spiritual superstars.

It matters a great deal, therefore, that average people emerge as champions and overcomers through the midst of their trials and difficulties. Will you be an end-time hero with the lowly heart of a bond-servant? Time will tell; I believe you can.

PROBING QUESTIONS

What are some of the temptations that Daniel would have faced? How do they relate to the temptations we face in our day?

How has the spiritual superstar mentality exacted a heavy toll on the modern church?

What is the value of learning the confidence of a king, but with the heart of a bond-servant?

ACTION STEP

Read the book of Daniel, drawing as many parallels to our current times as you can find.

CLOSING PRAYER

Dear Lord, I thank You that Your eternal kingdom is drawing near. Please help this fact to become a reality in the very depths of my heart!

FURTHER READING

Daniel 2:1-45; Luke 21:25-36; Galatians 1:10; Hebrews 12:25-29

CHAPTER FIFTY-TWO
EEYORE, HERO OF THE FAITH?

Our roads through the wilderness will end at the throne, all in God's time.

—Iverna Tompkins, speaker and author

And Jacob was left alone. And a man wrestled with him until the breaking of the day. When the man saw that he did not prevail against Jacob, he touched his hip socket, and Jacob's hip was put out of joint as he wrestled with him. Then he said, "Let me go, for the day has broken." But Jacob said, "I will not let you go unless you bless me." And he said to him, "What is your name?" And he said, "Jacob." Then he said, "Your name shall no longer be called Jacob, but Israel, for you have striven with God and with men, and have prevailed."

GENESIS 32:24-28 (ESV)

Young children love Winnie-the-Pooh and his faithful group of friends. Personally, I've always enjoyed Eeyore—that old, grey donkey who manages to find a pessimistic slant to every imaginable situation. If anyone could make a sunny day gloomy, it would be Eeyore. But in spite of his negative outlook on life, Eeyore has never ceased to be Pooh's faithful companion.

In his famous survey of the "heroes of the faith" (Hebrews 11), the writer of Hebrews provides powerful insights into the nature of a New Covenant relationship with God. Intentionally focusing on the strengths of these great men and women of God, he seems to ignore the major character flaws that so many of them displayed.

I sometimes think that the book's author had a difficult time putting a positive spin on the life of Jacob—an Old Testament Eeyore if ever there was one. Jacob, the deceiver, managed to highlight the negative in every situation, expressing fear far more than faith in his outlook on life. In stark contrast to his grandfather, Abraham, Jacob's accolade in Hebrews 11 amounted to but one verse—and even that spoke of his death. And yet, somehow, Jacob is still mentioned as a hero of the faith, considered by many to be one of the great patriarchs of Israel. In fact, the very name "Israel" stems from Jacob's wrestling match with God.

Rather than taking offense at Jacob's inclusion as a hero of the faith, I tend to find great solace. How comforting it is to know that God could take such a flawed person and leave such an amazing legacy. Not one of us is beyond hope!

Years ago, while preparing to launch into campus ministry, Debi and I strongly sensed that God was calling us to a narrow path—an unpaved trail that would require a significant measure of faith. Recognizing my extreme weakness in this area, I began to read the works of George Mueller and Hudson Taylor—Christian leaders who had a reputation for being men of faith.

George Mueller founded and managed (with no guaranteed income) five English orphanages simply by praying and trusting God for daily provision. Other than some struggles early in his life, Mueller navigated a host of faith challenges with ease, in spite of going through long seasons of intense need. Mueller's contemporary, Hudson Taylor, made his own massive impact on the world while serving as a missionary to inland China during the 1800s, but his experience was very different than that of Mueller's. Hudson Taylor struggled with unbelief for a much longer period of time and yet moved forward regardless, his heart filled with a vision to touch that great nation for Christ.

While the lessons from Mueller's life inspired me to trust God more, I felt somewhat alienated from his experience because of his apparent lack of struggle. "I have so many doubts," I thought, "I can never be anything like him." Hudson Taylor's story, on the contrary, was more in line with my own experience. The example Taylor set by overcoming his personal weaknesses encouraged me to press on in my service to God, in spite of my own weaknesses and struggles.

When God grows spiritual champions, He never utilizes a rubber stamp of conformity. Instead, He meets every person where he or she happens to be at a given moment, carefully crafting a personalized plan—usually including a wilderness experience or two—for growth. In the end, what makes such a champion is not a high level of ability or personal charisma. No, qualities such as faithfulness, courage, tenacity, and persistence serve as the raw materials from which our heavenly Father can produce a lasting legacy.

I am now convinced that Jacob deserves to be among the heroes of our faith—not simply because of his physical lineage, but because he laid hold of God and refused to let go. No one knew of his unworthiness more than Jacob himself; he was acutely aware of how far he fell short of his grandfather Abraham's standard of faith and courage. Yet, in his own way, Jacob proved to be a courageous champion. Choosing not to disqualify himself because of his unworthiness, Jacob laid hold of God's blessings and promises with an ironlike grip. Ironically, this pessimistic Eeyore has left footsteps in which we would do well to travel.

Personally, I hope that when all is dark and God appears to be absent, I will persist in the same way that Jacob did. When those around me become hardened, or turn aside to follow their own ways, I want to courageously march on in the things of God. I deeply desire to remain faithful to our King who is worthy of such faithfulness. Perhaps, when my time on this earth comes to an end, my life's epitaph will say only: "He faithfully persisted." That would be enough.

As we come to the end of our wilderness season together, I want to encourage you to faithfully and courageously persist in your pursuit of God, tenaciously laying hold of His faithful promises regardless of your personal shortcomings, or the state of the world around you. In due season, you will emerge a champion in your own right, for there is no such thing as a great man or woman of God—only a great God who reveals His glory through weak and imperfect human vessels. If God can cause His greatness to shine through Jacob's flawed life, certainly He can do the same through yours and mine!

PROBING QUESTIONS

How does the Hebrews 11 focus on the strengths of the heroes of the faith relate to the essence of the New Covenant as found in Hebrews 8:8-12?

What encourages you about Jacob's example?

Why are virtues such as courage and persistence so important to all of us?

ACTION STEP

True learning and growth come by repetition. Get out your calendar and make plans to go through this devotional again at some point in the future.

CLOSING PRAYER

Heavenly Father, I thank You so much for Your patient grace! Help me to persist in my pursuit of You for all of my days. My deep desire is to emerge from the wilderness as a champion for Christ's honor!

FURTHER READING

Genesis 32; Luke 18:1-8; Hebrews 8:8-12

APPENDIX I
INSPIRATIONAL BIBLE PASSAGES
AND PROMISES

A thorough knowledge of the Bible is worth more than a college education.
                    –Theodore Roosevelt, 26th President of the United States

---

So Jesus was saying to those Jews who had believed Him, "If you continue in My word, then you are truly disciples of Mine; and you will know the truth, and the truth will make you free."

JOHN 8:31-32 (NASB)

Below is a small sampling of Bible verses I find inspirational. All passages are from the updated New American Standard Version (NASB) because that is the translation I normally read and study.

There are many verses that we would do well to memorize in an effort to renew our minds and to establish God's truth in our hearts. Memorizing Scripture can be immensely helpful, so it is best to find one particular translation as your primary reading Bible.

Those who have not yet settled on a favorite translation can ask for recommendations from seasoned Christians and/or do some online research. In choosing a Bible, we are concerned with both accuracy *and* readability. The Bible versions which have a more literal, word for word, translation are generally more reliable, but can sometimes be more difficult to read. Thus, the best translation for you as an individual will be the most literal version that fits with your personal reading ability.

My personal recommendations according to reading level are:

English Translation	Approximate Grade Reading Level
New American Standard (NASB)	11
English Standard Version (ESV)	9-10
New King James Version (NKJV)	8-9
Holman Christian Standard (HCSB)	7-8
New International Version (NIV)	7-8
New English Translation (NET)	7

I am not saying that all versions excluded from this list are bad. I simply want to provide a good starting point for those who may be new to the Bible. Your next step would be to pull up each version on the internet (or borrow a hard copy) and spend some time reading the text until you find a translation that you feel comfortable using.

INSPIRATIONAL SCRIPTURE PASSAGES

The LORD is my shepherd,
I shall not want.
He makes me lie down in green pastures;
He leads me beside quiet waters.
He restores my soul;
He guides me in the paths of righteousness
For His name's sake.
Even though I walk through the valley of the shadow of death,
I fear no evil, for You are with me;
Your rod and Your staff, they comfort me.
You prepare a table before me in the presence of my enemies;
You have anointed my head with oil;
My cup overflows.
Surely goodness and lovingkindness will follow me all the days of my life,
And I will dwell in the house of the LORD forever. Psalms 23

For His anger is but for a moment,
His favor is for a lifetime;
Weeping may last for the night,
But a shout of joy comes in the morning. Psalms 30:5

Many are the afflictions of the righteous,
But the LORD delivers him out of them all. Psalms 34:19

A father of the fatherless and a judge for the widows,
Is God in His holy habitation. Psalms 68:5

As far as the east is from the west,
So far has He removed our transgressions from us. Psalms 103:12

Your word I have treasured in my heart,
That I may not sin against You. Psalms 119:11

Your word is a lamp to my feet
And a light to my path. Psalms 119:105

Trust in the LORD with all your heart
And do not lean on your own understanding.
In all your ways acknowledge Him,
And He will make your paths straight. Proverbs 3:5-6

But the path of the righteous is like the light of dawn,
That shines brighter and brighter until the full day. Proverbs 4:18

A righteous man who walks in his integrity—
How blessed are his sons after him. Proverbs 20:7

Those who wait for the LORD
Will gain new strength;
They will mount up with wings like eagles,
They will run and not get tired,
They will walk and not become weary. Isaiah 40:31

"For I know the plans that I have for you," declares the LORD, "plans for welfare and not for calamity to give you a future and a hope. Then you will call upon Me and come and pray to Me, and I will listen to you. You will seek Me and find Me when you search for Me with all your heart." Jeremiah 29:11-13

Behold, as for the proud one,
His soul is not right within him;
But the righteous will live by his faith. Habakkuk 2:4

"Come to Me, all who are weary and heavy-laden, and I will give you rest. Take My yoke upon you and learn from Me, for I am gentle and humble in heart, and YOU WILL FIND REST FOR YOUR SOULS. For My yoke is easy and My burden is light." Matthew 11:28-30

"Do not be afraid, little flock, for your Father has chosen gladly to give you the kingdom." Luke 12:32

Therefore there is now no condemnation for those who are in Christ Jesus. Romans 8:1

For you have not received a spirit of slavery leading to fear again, but you have received a spirit of adoption as sons by which we cry out, "Abba! Father!" Romans 8:15

And we know that God causes all things to work together for good to those who love God, to those who are called according to His purpose. Romans 8:28

For I am convinced that neither death, nor life, nor angels, nor principalities, nor things present, nor things to come, nor powers, nor height, nor depth, nor any other created thing, will be able to separate us from the love of God, which is in Christ Jesus our Lord. Romans 8:38-39

Do not be overcome by evil, but overcome evil with good. Romans 12:21

And He has said to me, "My grace is sufficient for you, for power is perfected in weakness." Most gladly, therefore, I will rather boast about my weaknesses, so that the power of Christ may dwell in me. 2 Corinthians 12:9

For by grace you have been saved through faith; and that not of yourselves, it is the gift of God; not as a result of works, so that no one may boast. For we are His workmanship, created in Christ Jesus for good works, which God prepared beforehand so that we would walk in them. Ephesians 2:8-10

Now to Him who is able to do far more abundantly beyond all that we ask or think, according to the power that works within us, to Him be the glory in the church and in Christ Jesus to all generations forever and ever. Amen. Ephesians 3:20-21

For I am confident of this very thing, that He who began a good work in you will perfect it until the day of Christ Jesus. Philippians 1:6

Be anxious for nothing, but in everything by prayer and supplication with thanksgiving let your requests be made known to God. And the peace of God, which surpasses all comprehension, will guard your hearts and your minds in Christ Jesus. Philippians 4:6-7

Therefore, since we have a great high priest who has passed through the heavens, Jesus the Son of God, let us hold fast our confession. For we do not have a high priest who cannot sympathize with our weaknesses, but One who has been tempted in all things as we are, yet without sin. Therefore let us draw near with confidence to the throne of grace, so that we may receive mercy and find grace to help in time of need. Hebrews 4:14-16

And without faith it is impossible to please Him, for he who comes to God must believe that He is and that He is a rewarder of those who seek Him. Hebrews 11:6

But if any of you lacks wisdom, let him ask of God, who gives to all generously and without reproach, and it will be given to him. James 1:5

Grace and peace be multiplied to you in the knowledge of God and of Jesus our Lord; seeing that His divine power has granted to us everything pertaining to life and godliness, through the true knowledge of Him who called us by His own glory and excellence. For by these He has granted to us His precious and magnificent promises, so that by them you may become partakers of the divine nature, having escaped the corruption that is in the world by lust. 2 Peter 1:2-4

If we confess our sins, He is faithful and righteous to forgive us our sins and to cleanse us from all unrighteousness. 1 John 1:9

You are from God, little children, and have overcome them; because greater is He who is in you than he who is in the world. 1 John 4:4

For this is the love of God, that we keep His commandments; and His commandments are not burdensome. For whatever is born of God overcomes the world; and this is the victory that has overcome the world—our faith. 1 John 5:3-4

APPENDIX II
HOW TO JOIN THE FAMILY OF GOD

The story of paradise lost becoming paradise regained is the story of God's grace bringing us from alienation from him to membership in his family. God's grace restores us to what Adam lost for us—sonship to the God who made us, loves us, and provides for us in every detail in life.
–Sinclair B. Ferguson, pastor and scholar

"For I know the plans that I have for you," declares the LORD, "plans for welfare and not for calamity to give you a future and a hope." Then you will call upon Me and come and pray to Me, and I will listen to you. You will seek Me and find Me when you search for Me with all your heart.
JEREMIAH 29:11-13 (NASB)

WHAT DOES IT MEAN TO BE A CHRISTIAN?

One of the problems we face is that the term *Christian* has been given such a broad meaning that it now means very little. Almost anyone who professes even a vague belief in God is now considered to be a Christian. Many have grown up attending church and professing Christ but having little desire to adhere to His teachings. Others have made some type of a decision to receive Christ but with no resulting life-change. Virtually all of these people would call themselves Christians, but are they really followers of Christ if they only give lip service to His teachings?

One would think that after 2000 years we'd have this all figured out, but many of us still struggle to grasp the true nature of

Christianity. This is not due to any shortcoming on God's part, but it does speak volumes about the wayward tendencies of the human race. What makes a person a Christian? Being baptized at birth? Having a religious upbringing? Going to church? Saying a prayer? Celebrating communion? Reading the Bible? Having a spiritual experience?

THE BLOOD COVENANT

A key concept that is often forgotten in many Christian circles is that of the *blood covenant*. Virtually synonymous with the ancient idea of a *blood brotherhood*, a blood covenant is *a sacred and binding relationship*. It speaks of a relational oneness of the highest order. When two individuals (or groups) joined together in a covenant relationship, their friends, enemies, possessions, and identities became shared. To enter a covenant often brought excellent benefits; to break a covenant resulted in many painful and terrible curses. A covenant is to be regarded with the seriousness of the weightiest relationship and celebrated as the most blessed.

The failure to understand the nature of a covenant unleashes a torrent of doubt, and, inevitably, the inability to understand how God interacts with humanity. God's promises are not indiscriminate words intended for anyone with a casual interest; they are given to His covenant children.

THE PROBLEM OF PRIDE

From the beginning of time as we know it, God created the human race to share an intimate, covenant relationship with Him. However, in eating from the tree of the knowledge of good and evil, humankind chose a path of independence, essentially seeking to be like God apart from God. Really, it was—and still is—all about self-focused pride. We each want to be the center of our own universe. We seek to control our lives, our circumstances, and even the lives of others. And, of course, a primary human quest is that of personal glory—to establish a sense of goodness and significance apart from the God who created us.

These three root motivations—self-centeredness, self-sovereignty (or self-will) and self-glorification—combine to create the massive, painful problem we call the "human condition". Humanism, at least to a degree, delights in these pursuits, seeing little wrong with them, except in their extreme forms. Most religions promise hope and meaning through various means of self-effort such as attending meetings, giving money, doing good deeds, etc. Biblical Christianity alone teaches that we can be free from the ingrained motivation of pride (and its resulting consequences) only through the gospel of Jesus Christ.

THE GOOD NEWS OF THE GOSPEL

Although equal to God the Father, Jesus humbled Himself to become a man. He was miraculously born to a virgin so that, as a human, He might model a covenant relationship with His heavenly Father. Jesus then died as the perfect sacrifice for all sins so that all humans could have the opportunity to enter into the *New Covenant in His blood* (see 1 Corinthians 11:25).

Becoming a Christian is not simply about making a decision for Christ, or seeking forgiveness so that we can avoid the punishment of hell. It's not even about asking Him into our hearts so that we can have better lives. The Christian life is one of radical transformation, not self-improvement.

All too often, the sovereign King of the Universe is seen as a giant Santa Claus in the sky who is obligated to meet our selfish expectations. The true gospel proclaims the opposite, calling us from our self-centered independence to a full dependence on God. The gospel is both a call to surrender our desire/need for control to His will, and to seek our sense of goodness through our relationship with Him, rather than through self-effort.

Salvation is by faith. Do you believe that Jesus is God eternal? That He lowered Himself to become a man, being born into this world through a virgin? That, although Jesus was without sin, He died a horrible death on the cross, willingly taking upon Himself the curses of covenant breakers such as ourselves? Jesus paid the steepest of prices as a substitute for our failures so that we might be freely— and fully—forgiven of all our sins. The story doesn't end there! On the third day, Jesus rose from the dead, shattering the powers of sin and death. No force from earth, or from hell, could keep Him down!

The Bible teaches that those who enter into the New Covenant through faith in Christ become the true children of God. Eternal life is about getting to know Him, not about obeying lists of rules, or simply trying to reach a final destination. God has always encouraged humankind to seek His face, to search out His truths, and to turn to His ways. Our eternal Father is ever willing to reveal Himself to those who choose to humble their hearts before Him. He stands not as a drill sergeant ready to hammer us, but as the all-knowing Creator who always seeks our good.

TURNING FROM THE OLD TO THE NEW

The Christian life operates by faith because it is the only known antidote for self-exalting pride. Without trust, relational intimacy with God is impossible. All of humankind is being called to *repent*, that is, *to turn from our idolatry, self-centeredness, self-sovereignty, and self-glorification to a life of faith.* Faith calls us to put Him first above all others in our life, to surrender ourselves to Him as Lord, and to find our source of goodness and righteousness through our relationship with the heavenly Father.

> *Now when they heard this, they were pierced to the heart, and said to Peter and the rest of the apostles, "Brethren, what shall we do?" Peter said to them, "Repent, and each of you be baptized in the name of Jesus Christ for the forgiveness of your sins; and you will receive the gift of the Holy Spirit. For the promise is for you and your children and for all who are far off, as many as the Lord our God will call to Himself." Acts 2:37-39 (NASB)*

BECOMING A CHRISTIAN

For the early church, entering into a New Covenant relationship through Christ was signified by the covenant ceremony of *water baptism*. Getting water baptized was like getting married to God— it was the time when a public confession of a person's faith and devotion were proclaimed. The individual was immersed under water, signifying the cleansing of sins and the burial of the old, independent self. He or she was then raised up by another person's power into the resurrection life of Christ. Finally, the covenant relationship with God was sealed as the Holy Spirit (God Himself) filled and empowered each new believer.

It was at this point that the covenant promise of Jeremiah 29:11-13 became a reality in their lives. God was in them and would always be with them. All that was theirs was His, and all that was His became theirs. And with the barrier of sin removed, God was free to work all of their negative circumstances toward His good purposes.

Certainly, times have changed and so has the manner in which people interpret the Christian faith. But covenant relationships are enduring—meaning that God's overall design and plan has not changed since the days of the early Christian church. God's covenant promises remain in effect for our day. Each of us has the opportunity to enter into a uniquely sacred and enduring relationship with the Creator of the Universe.

Our modern perspective of the salvation experience is disjointed. We pray the sinner's prayer one day, contemplate maybe getting baptized some time down the road, and then argue about what it means to be filled with the Holy Spirit. God is gracious and allows us to be saved in this manner, but it is comparable to operating a high performance sports car on only one or two cylinders. It simply does not work very well—as evidenced by the current state of Western church.

Becoming a member of God's covenant family is not an obligation, but rather a tremendous honor and privilege. I believe we do tremendous disservice—and even damage—to the cause of the gospel when we try to beg and manipulate others into the Christian faith. Therefore, I will not plead with you, the reader, to become a Christian.

If the message of the Christian gospel somehow resonates with your heart, it means that the Creator of the Universe is personally drawing you toward Himself. If you desire to know God, to experience His forgiveness and saving grace, and to be adopted into

His royal family, then I encourage you to take some time right now to cry out to your loving Father in heaven, fully surrendering your heart to Him. Please *don't* take this step unless you are serious about being "all in". A blood covenant relationship will allow for nothing less.

Your next steps would be to make an immediate effort to find a healthy local gathering of Christians and to get water baptized. (You may have noticed that you cannot water baptize yourself!) I freely admit that unhealthy churches abound, but there are definitely some great ones out there—ask God to guide you. (Appendix III was added to help you with your search.)

If you are not yet ready to become a Christian, but are considering the possibility, then I would advise you to explore the Christian faith more thoroughly. You would do well to pray something similar to the following, "Heavenly Father, if You are there, I want to know You. Please open my eyes to Your reality and my heart to Your ways. Guide me in my search for truth and open up to me a new world that I never knew existed."

Regardless of how far along in our faith journey any of us happen to be, there is so much more that awaits us. Even the most advanced believer has only begun to taste of who God is and of all that He has for us. Let's be wise enough to wholeheartedly seek His face, surrender our desires, and give ourselves in service to His eternal plans and purposes. In the end, those who take such an approach will have very few regrets.

APPENDIX III
TIPS TO HELP FIND A LOCAL CHURCH

I heard of a man who said to the preacher, "I want to sing in your choir." The preacher replied, "But you don't belong here. Where do you have your membership?" He said, "I don't belong to any local church. I belong to the invisible church." The pastor said, "Then I suggest that you join the invisible choir."

–Vance Havner, preacher and author

And they devoted themselves to the apostles' teaching, to the fellowship, to the breaking of bread, and to the prayers.
ACTS 2:42 (HCSB)

Technically, there is only one church (with many different expressions that we call "churches") in a community. Finding a good local church to connect with will greatly enrich our Christian experience, but the search can sometimes be quite challenging. To help with this process, I have provided a few tips that you may find beneficial. Please understand that these are general guidelines according to what I think is important; they are not intended to be conclusive or comprehensive instructions. It is important that you seek God's guidance for yourself, taking the time to thoroughly investigate your options.

In many parts of the world, the traditional definition of a church has focused more on buildings and rituals. Thankfully, this mindset has been called into question in recent years. To be painfully honest, even many growing churches in the Western world bear little resemblance to the New Testament church as seen in the book of Acts.

The second chapter of Mark records an experience in which Jesus was challenged by the Pharisees regarding obedience to Sabbath rituals. We would do well to apply Christ's classic response to our perspective of the local church.

> *Jesus said to them, "The Sabbath was made for man, and not man for the Sabbath."* Mark 2:27 (NASB)

In a similar way, the local church was made for humans, and not humans for the local church. The goal is not to squeeze ourselves into a precast mold but to live and grow together in vital relationships. Corresponding to this, I think that Ephesians 4 provides an excellent overview of what a local church should be about.

> *And He gave some as apostles, and some as prophets, and some as evangelists, and some as pastors and teachers, for the equipping of the saints for the work of service, to the building up of the body of Christ; until we all attain to the unity of the faith, and of the knowledge of the Son of God, to a mature man, to the measure of the stature which belongs to the fullness of Christ. As a result, we are no longer to be children, tossed here and there by waves and carried about by every wind of doctrine, by the trickery of men, by craftiness in deceitful scheming; but speaking the truth in love, we are to grow up in all aspects into Him who is the head, even Christ, from whom the whole body, being fitted and held together by what every joint supplies, according to the proper working of each individual part, causes the growth of the body for the building up of itself in love.* Ephesians 4:11-16 (NASB)

In other words, I would be more concerned about the life and fruit of a particular gathering of Christians than I would about the exact form of their structure. This is not to say that structure is unimportant, but that your primary reason to get involved with a local fellowship is to connect with a group of believers who will encourage each other toward maturity in Christ and collectively serve God's purposes together.

As it should be with finding a spouse, you shouldn't blind yourself to major character deficiencies through the "dating process", but neither should you expect everything to be exactly as you wish. Remember, the goal is to find a local fellowship where God is calling you to connect with spiritually maturing Christians. In most cases, this will also be a place that you feel you can call home. Because a church consists of imperfect people, you will never find the perfect church. If you do locate one, it will no longer be perfect after you join!

Prayer, of course, is the best starting place. God's wisdom and knowledge far exceed ours, and so we want to ask Him to guide our search. What we desire in our hearts, or see with our natural eyes, may not always be what is best. Surrendering our desires to Him and remaining sensitive to the Holy Spirit are vital to this process.

Because our efforts to follow God's leading are imperfect, I suggest that you take a few practical steps to help you more readily identify a healthy church—as opposed to one that may actually be detrimental to your spiritual well-being.

1. Try doing an internet search to familiarize yourself with the churches in your area. The majority of churches in our day and age will have a website or, at the very least, be listed in some sort of directory. Through the website, you can usually view their statement of faith (list of doctrinal beliefs) and possibly get a sense of what they value. I say "possibly" because, as with an online dating service, a church website may simply present what they think people want to see.

In an ideal world, the best church for you would be the closest. We don't live in an ideal world. You may need to travel a little to find a local fellowship that works well for you. If transportation is available, and you have the means, don't be afraid to expand the scope beyond your immediate vicinity.

2. An appropriate next step would be to ask questions of those you know to be Christ-like Christians. If you don't know of anyone, talk to neighbors, coworkers, or anyone else you might know in your community. I suggest that you not limit your efforts to just one or two opinions. Perspectives are so diverse that it is always best to look for trends. If, for example, four out of five people you respect have a positive impression of Living Waters Fellowship, then it is probably worth checking out.

3. Make a list of churches you would like to visit. It wouldn't hurt to contact them to confirm service times and to ask about their dress codes. If visiting a church makes you nervous, not knowing what to wear will make it that much more difficult.

4. When visiting a church, plan to arrive fifteen to twenty minutes early so that you can look around and ask questions. Some churches have information desks. Many provide an opportunity for visitors to meet people after the service. Don't be afraid to take advantage of these opportunities to ask questions. Always ask questions.

Even if you really like the first church you attend, it may be worth visiting some of the others in the community. When you eventually face difficulties in your new church home—and you will—you'll want to be confident that you are in the right place. Don't be afraid to visit a church more than once.

5. There are some specific things to discern when checking out a local church and reviewing their doctrine. Do they hold a high view of the Bible, seeing it as the inspired word of God and the authority for Christian living? Is the worship God-centered and does it resonate with you? Do you sense that the leaders are humble, as opposed to being self-centered? Does the

environment of the service feel free? Pastors will always try to persuade people to action—it is part of their job—but steer clear of any church that comes across as manipulating or controlling. Do the people appear to be warm and inviting? Is there spiritual vitality within the church, or is the atmosphere dry and lifeless?

6. A few important questions should be asked. One of the most important issues will be their perspective of law and grace. If a church has a lot of written (or unwritten) rules, any mention of grace will be shallow. On the other hand, how we live does matter, so if *grace* is interpreted to be *the freedom to do whatever people want*, there is a problem.

It is also important to find out about their perspective of the covenant unity of the body of Christ, including how they relate to other churches in the community. A healthy church should have healthy relationships with other local churches. Steer clear of a church that comes across as elitist, or that isolates itself from other Christians in the community. Finally, ask about the primary vision of the church, what programs may be applicable to you (and your family), how you might be able to connect with people, and any potential opportunities for service.

7. Once you find a church you feel good about, attend for at least two or three months before you consider becoming a member and serving in any significant way. You just want to be sure that it is a good fit for you.

As stated previously, there is no such thing as a perfect church, and so it is likely that you will like some things and not others. In the end, what you need to know is that the church is a good place to grow spiritually, that you (and your family) fit fairly well, and, ultimately, that it is the place God is calling you to land.

Once you firmly decide which local body of believers God is leading you to join, by all means get involved. Don't feel obligated to do everything, but find your niche and be faithful to what God is calling you to do. If it is a healthy environment, you will be blessed with rich relationships, solid spiritual growth, and an opportunity to impact our world in a meaningful way!

ABOUT THE AUTHOR

Having had very little religious involvement before his college years, Bob Santos became a Christian in the spring of 1980 while attending Indiana University of Pennsylvania (IUP), from which he graduated in 1982 with a Bachelor of Science degree in Chemistry. Upon coming to Christ, Bob fully involved himself with various aspects of ministry. After meeting and marrying the love of his life (Debi), Bob proceeded to attempt to do all of the things that a "good" Christian is expected to do. The newlyweds found a local church, got heavily involved, and served in just about every imaginable capacity—except for the worship team. (Even spiritual endeavors have natural limitations!)

Along the way, Bob became frustrated. He didn't feel as though they were seeing any significant fruit from all of their hard work, nor did he feel that his own walk with God was near what it should have been. Externally, he saw far too many church attenders whose measure of spiritual maturity appeared to be far below what it should have been considering the length of time they had been Christians. Internally, he felt dry and spiritually parched in spite of all of his Christian activity. Effective solutions to these problems, it seemed, were nearly impossible to come by. Two very important things followed.

First, Bob began to cry out to God for answers to his personal struggles. The result? The Holy Spirit began to reveal a deeper understanding of the root issues that were plaguing Bob's spiritual well-being. Unbelief, idolatry, insecurity, and a need to be in control were some of the primary reasons that his version of Christianity wasn't working all that well. As Bob began to make personal adjustments based on what God was teaching him, the spiritual dimension of his life began to improve dramatically.

Second, Bob and Debi sensed the Spirit's leading to become involved with their church's campus outreach to IUP. They stepped on campus with a vision to help prepare a generation of college students to both serve in local churches, and to impact the world through their vocations. Utilizing what he had learned through his own personal struggles, Bob developed a Bible study that he named *Freedom in Christ*. Through the years that followed, the *Freedom in Christ* Bible study became a cornerstone of their college ministry efforts, making a huge impact on many young lives.

Having long held an intense concern for the well-being of the Western church, Bob felt compelled to take his teaching materials to a broader audience. The problem, however, was that no long-lasting doors of opportunity were opening. Finally, in the spring of 2006, Bob and Debi founded Search for Me Ministries, Inc. (SfMe Ministries) as a teaching ministry to serve the body of Christ at large. SfMe Media was later added with a focus on using published materials to help form and equip a generation of world changers for Christ. More information about the work of SfMe Ministries and its resources can be found at our website (www.searchforme.info) and on the next page.

Bob was licensed for ministry in 1997 and ordained in 2005 through Elim Fellowship (www.elimfellowship.org). He currently serves as Elim's southwestern Pennsylvania area representative.

ADDITIONAL RESOURCES FROM SEARCH FOR ME MINISTRIES

Additional copies of *Champions in the Wilderness* are available through our SfMe Media website (www.sfme.org) and at other points of distribution.

Our first production, *The Search for Me: A Journey Toward a Rock Solid Identity*, intended primarily for small group use, is a 12-part DVD study that boldly, but lovingly, touches many of the core issues that influence human behavior. This is not a casual study! The concepts presented will challenge old, unhealthy mindsets as they provide a powerful exposé of the human condition and Christianity's solution. The effects are multi-faceted as participants grow together in faith, renew their love for God, and break free from sin. The audio files of the series are free for streaming from our website for those who would like to review the study before purchasing.

You will want to stay tuned as SfMe Ministries publishes additional books in the coming years!

DONATING TO SEARCH FOR ME MINISTRIES

We are a *faith ministry*, meaning that we seek to put our focus on God as our provider and do not aggressively solicit contributions. "Opportunity without pressure" is our motto when it comes to raising the necessary funds to fulfill our vision of forming and equipping a generation of world changers. Those whose hearts move them to give financially are more than welcome to join us in advancing God's kingdom—the resources will be put to good use. We will not distribute your contact information, nor will we continually badger you to give more. More information about financial partnership can be found on our ministry website. SfMe Ministries is an IRS recognized 501(c)(3) non-profit organization.

END NOTES

[1]Achtemeier, P. J., & Society of Biblical Literature. (1985). *Harper's Bible dictionary* (1st ed.) (1133). San Francisco: Harper & Row.

[2]If you have never fasted before, it is best to do a little research first so that your fast is truly beneficial rather than damaging. Those with medical problems or eating disorders should not fast from food without medical supervision. Those who are able to fast still need to exercise wisdom. Breaking a fast with a large pepperoni pizza, for example, will not make for a satisfying experience. Books on the subject of fasting are readily available.

[3]For those who may be unfamiliar with my somewhat warped sense of humor, this is a joke. I actually feel a very strong call to serve and influence the church in the U.S. Even in her weakened state, she still has tremendous influence (for good and bad) all over the world.

[4]J. Thomson, G. S. S. (1996). Rainbow. In D. R. W. Wood, I. H. Marshall, A. R. Millard, J. I. Packer & D. J. Wiseman (Eds.), New Bible dictionary (D. R. W. Wood, I. H. Marshall, A. R. Millard, J. I. Packer & D. J. Wiseman, Ed.) (3rd ed.) (1000). Leicester, England; Downers Grove, IL: InterVarsity Press.

[5]Josephus *Jewish Antiquities* 20.145-46